the UnWord

DICTIONARY

the UnWord
DICTIONARY

1000 Words
for Things You Didn't Think Had Words!

STEVE KIEHL

Marion Street Press, Inc.
Oak Park, Illinois, USA
www.marionstreetpress.com

Cover design and interior illustrations by Rick Menard

ISBN: 1-933338-19-9
ISBN-13: 978-1-933338-1-94
Printed in U.S.A.
Printing 10 9 8 7 6 5 4 3 2 1

Marion Street Press, Inc.
PO Box 2249
Oak Park, IL 60303
866-443-7987
www.marionstreetpress.com

Acknowledgments

I'd like to give my thanks to everyone who has helped in making all this possible. First, to my savior, Jesus; I wouldn't have come down this path without Him. To Ed Avis and the staff at Marion Street Press, whose interest and help have made this book possible. To Emily Moyer-Grice, who helped sift and proof all these wonderful entries. To my family, whose continued interest and support keeps me on track. To my friends, whose admiration and good humor have helped inspire what Unwords is now and what it will be in the future.

Finally, to all you fans and subscribers for your artistry in these creations and your continued use of these new words. Your knowledge and contributions have helped grow this living resource and have inspired young minds to discover new words themselves.

Introduction

Back in the fall semester of 2000, some college mates and I found ourselves continually combining or inventing words to express our ideas and actions. Maybe this was due to passing brain clouds, or perhaps it was because we were all engineers and scientists who knew far too much technobabble and very little of our own English language.

We conversed, we laughed, we thought up more words in our boredom. Eventually we started forgetting our gems of conversation, and soon, like any dot-com capitalist, I suggested, "We should have a website for this."

In a few months, Unwords.com was born. In its early days, with our low budget, the site crawled along, or not, thanks to our newfound knowledge of web development, or lack thereof. Our determination to keep things running pulled us through each mistake and growing pain.

In those Neanderthal days we reveled in our small Internet fame like anime characters with too large eyes staring at hit counters. Countless mentions across the web, in classrooms, on the radio, and in the news kept the orange and blue flying.

Every emo teen, dyslexic mis-speller, conjugal temptress, street-smart gangsta, philosophical anthropologist, and coffee-drinking hipster now joins us to make English their language. In this book you will find a selection from some of the most thoughtful, funny, and all around great words from our contributors.

I'm sure you will enjoy a good laugh and a smile in the following pages, and I welcome you to visit us and contribute your own thoughts to our community.

—Steve Kiehl

the UnWord DICTIONARY

# #

007 (dŭb'əl-ō-sĕv'ən)

(n.) A license to kill; used in medical terminology when someone makes a mistake.

Example: *"That incorrect dosage almost killed your patient!" says Dr. K. "Well, 007," replies the intern.*

112% (wŭn hŭn'drĭd twĕlv pər-sĕnt')

(adv.) Sarcastically. To achieve better results than what is possible; to exceed the best possible outcome.

Example: *"Mom, I'll clean my room 112%!"*

404 (fôr-ō-fôr)

(n.) A clueless person.

Example: *Don't bother asking him... He's 404, man.*

Origin: From the Web error message, "404: Not found," meaning that a requested page could not be located.

A

abandonmitt (ə-băn'dən-mĭt)

(n.) The act of abruptly letting go of someone's hand before they anticipated it.

Example: *Hey, don't abandonmitt me — it's freezing out here and I want to hold your hand.*

abbone (ăb-bō-nē)

(adj.) The agony or severe pain caused by attempting to stand or walk when a person's knees have seized up, primarily after a prolonged period of inactivity. Most commonly suffered by travelers using trains, cars, and planes as methods of transportation.

Origin: A corruption of the words *agony* and *bone*.

abbreveil (ə-brē'vāl')

(v.) To shorten words to a point where no meaning can be construed from them.

abdicake (ăb'dĭ-kāk)

(v.) To give up the last piece of cake to someone else.

Example: "*Is anyone going to eat the last piece of cake?*" "*I was, but I'll abdicake in your favor.*"

Origin: The contraction of the words *abdicate*, to relinquish power, and *cake*.

abolical (ə-bŏ'lĭ-kəl)

(adj.) Something loathsome or unusually cruel, perhaps associated with dire misfortune.

Origin: From *diabolical*, something of wickedness and evil, and *abhor* or *abominate*.

abominaball (ə-bŏm'ə-nə-bôl)

(n.) Any ball that has made its way into the interior of a greenhouse or home by exploiting the presence of an unopened window.

Origin: From *abominable* and *ball*.

accidue (ăk'sĭ-dü)

(n.) Small pieces of broken glass, metal, and other debris that remain at the scene of an accident for months after.

Note: Also called *smashal*

acknodledge (ăk-nŏd-'lĭj)

(v.) To nod at someone walking in the opposite direction while avoiding a conversation.

Origin: From *acknowledge* and *nod*.

acluistic (ā-clü'ĭst-ĭc)

(adj.) Describing or pertaining to anything clueless; without a clue.

adjectize (aj'ĭk-tīz')

(v.) To describe thoroughly with an excessive, and often unnecessary, number of words.

adminisphere (ăd-mĭn'ĭs-fĭr')

(n.) The levels of management where big, impractical, and counterproductive decisions are made.

Example: *The administration decided to replace all 700 of our servers with three mainframes. I'm telling you, their brains don't get enough air in that adminisphere.*

adoricious (ăd'ə-rĭsh'əs)

(adj.) The quality of being able to be adored. Used in place of "adorable," which tends to imply cuteness as opposed to the ability to be adored. Useful when subject or a quality of the subject is endearing, but not necessarily cute.

accumulotion (ə-kyüm'yə-lō'shən)
    (n.) The uncomfortably grotesque layer of slime that adorns
    the opening of a lotion dispenser.

adultish (ə-dŭlt'ĭsh)
    (adj.) Closely resembling an adult person.

    Example: *That responsible teen is very adultish.*

adverteasement (ăd-vər-tēz'mənt)

(n.) Any sexual representation used for the purpose of obtaining an individual or group's attention. Often used in media outlets.

advomentary (ăd-və-men'tən-rē)

(n.) An advocacy documentary motion picture. An advomentary uses documentary production styles to promote a specific opinion or "spin."

aesthete's foot (ĕs-thēts fut)

(n.) The chronic condition whereby one's socks match one's shirt without fail.

Origin: From *aesthetic*, something artistic or pleasing, and *athlete's foot*, a contagious fungal infection.

aggravistle (ăg'rə-vĭs'əl)

(n.) The small and inaccessible piece of steak that clings between the teeth and refuses to budge despite constant agitation, causing discomfort and extreme annoyance.

Origin: From *aggravate*, to annoy or bother, and *gristle*, the cartilage in meat, which can get stuck between one's teeth.

aggravitch (ăg'rə-vĭch)

(n.) An itch that that does not lessen with scratching but instead seems to spread to surrounding areas, causing annoyance and sometimes paranoia and self-mutilation.

Example: *This aggravitch is driving me crazy! Freakin' poison ivy!*

aggrieviate (ăg'grē'vē-āt')

(v.tr.) To make a burden heavier. To render (something) more likely to aggrieve.

Origin: From Latin *aggravare*, to make heavier, and *gravis*, heavy, grave.

agiliteeth (ə-jĭl'ĭ-tēth)

(n.) The skill of using dental floss to effectively clean the entire mouth. Often perfected by individuals with germ phobias.

air biscuit (âr bĭs'kĭt)

(n.) To pass gas in a concentrated form.

Example: *I can't believe you just floated an air biscuit in this car while the windows are closed!*

alarmisist (ə-lärm'əs-ĭst)

(n.) A person who causes alarm in others by direct conflict or by interjecting false conflict into a situation. Also known as an *Eeyorist*, akin to Winnie the Pooh's friend Eeyore.

alcologic (ăl'kə-lŏj'ĭk)

(n.) Logic that is only understood while one is inebriated. Or to justify everything by the use of alcohol as the basis for every problem, debate, or argument.

alcotholic (ăl'kə-thə'lĭk)

(n.) One who uses alcohol to excess to escape his rigid Catholic upbringing.

Alfred Hitchcook (ăl'frĭd hĭch-kuk)

(v.) To stab continuously at a block of frozen vegetables or other frozen food items to make them cook faster.

Origin: The combination of bloody meat cleavers and frozen vegetables.

allergivate (ă'lĕrjĭvāt')

(v.) The inevitable action of cats and dogs to constantly gravitate toward guests who are allergic to them.

allergize (ăl'ə'r-jīz)

(v.) To cause your allergies to act up.

Example: *The fresh grass clippings are allergizing my eyes.*

Origin: From *allergy,* a sensitive reaction to a certain stimulus, and *energize,* to charge up.

alliterate (ā-lĭt-ər-ĭt)

(adj.) Having the ability to read but choosing not to. Not to be mistaken with those who are illiterate.

alphageek (ăl'fə-gēk)

(n.) The most knowledgeable, technically proficient person in an office or work group. Often found shunning lesser geeks in their cubicles.

Example: *I can't figure out what's wrong with this program. Get the alphageek to look at it.*

Origin: A technical form of the word *alpha male*, a dominant male figure.

aluminum ghetto (ə-lü'mə-nəm gĕt'ō)

(n.) A term used to describe a trailer park, usually in a poor, unkempt condition.

aluminumish (ə-lü'mə-nəm'ĭsh)

(adj.) Anything that looks like, is made of, or resembles aluminum.

amazorize (ə-māz'ə-rīz)

(v.) To make amazing or more amazing.

Example: *He amazorized his math grade with hard work and studying.*

ambiportalous (ăm-bĭ-pôr'tl'əs)

(adj.) Possessing the uncanny knack for approaching a set of double doors and always pushing the locked one.

Example: *I am impressed with how ambiportalous you are. That's the third wrong door you've pushed tonight.*

ambisextrous (ām'bĭ-sĕk'strəs)

(adj.) The feeling towards a person who has a strong attachment or attraction towards you when you have no definitive romantic feelings towards that person.

2. (adj.) In a romantic situation, the sense that one could say yes or no without feeling strongly in either direction.

Example: *"So, how was your date with the woman you met on the singles' site?" "Well, I'm a little ambisextrous. She was hot, but our politics are completely out of synch."*

ambivalate (ăm-bĭv'ə-lāt')

(v.) To play devil's advocate. Acting out ambivalence.

Origin: A verb form of *ambivalence*, playing both sides of a situation.

2. (v.) To vacillate between two opposing desires, impulses or decisions.

Example: *He's ambivalating between marrying Susie and riding his bike around the world.*

ambulament (ăm'byə-lə'mənt)

(n.) The excitement men experience when they hear a siren, often triggering hopes of a chaotic scene.

amsniffalent (ăm-snĭf'ə-lənt)

(adj.) Describing someone who doesn't cover his mouth when sneezing, thereby showing his willingness to share a cold with others.

Example: *Fred, if you insist on being so rudely amsniffalent, at least face away from me.*

analog-retentive (ăn'ə-lôg' rĭ-těn'tĭv)

(adj.) Describing antiquated computer systems, or those who have an undying love for them.

ancieverknowledgetale (ān-shěv'ər-nŏl'ĭj-tāl)

(n.) Any story about the "Good Old Days" told by an adult or other elderly person.

Origin: A contraction of the words *ancient*, *achiever*, *knowledge*, and *tale*, suggesting a tale from the knowledge of an ancient achiever.

animane (ăn'ə-măn)

(adj.) To treat animals with kindness and respect. Since animals aren't human, you can only treat them animanely, not humanely.

Origin: The contraction of the words *animal* and *humane*, treating humans in a dignified manner.

animositous (ăn'ə-mŏs'ĭ-təs)

(adj.) Describing the atmosphere between two people who do not like each other.

Example: *Relations between Jill and John have been distinctly animositous since she shot his cat.*

2. (adj.) Describing one's feelings or behavior toward someone one does not like.

Example: *I was feeling so animositous towards you, I could have screamed.*

annerving (ə-nûr-vĭng)

(adj.) Describing someone who is both annoying and getting on another's nerves. Beyond being a simple pest.

annoyitate (ə-noi'ə-tāt')

(v.tr.) Using one's ability to annoy and irritate at the same time.

anticappoint (ăn-tĭs'ə-point')

(v.tr.) To have a highly anticipated event fail to satisfy.

2. (v.tr.) To have high hopes met with disappointment.

anticillation (ăn-tĭs'l-ā'shən)

(n.) A feeling of anticipated superficial stimulation while waiting for something exciting to happen.

anticiprecipitate (ăn-tĭs'ə-prĭ-sĭp'ĭ-tāt')

(v.) Looking out a window persistently while anticipating a change in the weather that is to one's liking.

anticitickle (ăn'tĭs'əkl)

(v.) When one instinctively reacts to being tickled, before the tickle has actually occurred. Often, one is considered telepathically or telekinetically ticklish in cases like this.

2. (v.) When the anticipation of being tickled causes the afflicted to flinch and jerk around.

anticluistic (ăn'tē-klü'ĭs'tĭk)

(adj.) Describing a person who actively repels any attempt at getting a clue.

See also: *acluistic*

anticompanionize (ăn'tī-kəm-păn'yən-īz')

(v.) One's constant rejection of a boyfriend's or girlfriend's companion animal, or generally hating a partner's cat or dog for absolutely no reason at all.

antigravisnot (ăn'tē-grăv'ĭ-snŏt)

(n.) The ability of snot to run down one's face while his head is tilted back.

anxieapeek (ăng-zǐ'ĭ-pěk)

(n.) The cautious opening of an envelope containing semester grades or other possibly dangerous material.

apatheist (ap'ə–thě'tǐ–cǐst)

(n.) One who denies the possible existence of a supreme being only because he or she lacks interest in discovering this for him- or herself. Often mistaken with an atheist, who openly denies the existence of God or gods.

apatheticist (ap'ə thět'ǐ'ti–cǐst)

(n.) One who advocates apathy as the only logical response towards unanswerable questions or ineluctable problems.

apostrophascist (ə-pǒs'trə-fǎ'cǐst)

(n.) One of the army of self-righteous goons that jumps on others as soon as they veer even slightly away from the hideously outdated English grammar and punctuation standards laid down by the Victorians when they realized their mother tongue was mutated to the point that it would never have the elegance of Latin or the precision of High German.

appendasm (ə-pěn-dǎz'əm)

(n.) The twitching, uncomfortable sensation that passes through a limb when it is awakened from an appendoze. Appendasms may last for some time and can be quite intense depending on the length and depth of the appendoze.

appendoze (ə-pĕn-dōz)

(v.) The phenomena in which a part of the body seems to go to sleep. This is due to the body part having restricted blood flow for an extended period.

applicating (ăp'lĭ-kāt'ĭng)

(v.tr.) The act of submitting applications.

See also: *Bushism*

aristonaut (ə-rĭs'tə-nôt'')

(n.) Someone who bought his way into space with large amounts of money.

Origin: A conjunction of the words *astronaut* and *aristocrat*.

arrognorant (ăr'əg'nər-ənt)

(n.) A person who thinks he knows everything, but doesn't.

arrow-waster (ăr'ō-wā'stər)

(n.) One who does not immediately proceed when a left-turn arrow flashes green, preventing following motorists from making it through on the light.

Example: *If it wasn't for that arrow-waster yacking on her cell phone instead of watching the light, we would've been back to school in plenty of time.*

autocrappy (ô'tə-krăp'ē)

(adj.) Describing something that, although brand new, is unappealing or tasteless. Signifying an automatic categorization among poor products.

Example: *Almost everything found in the dirty bin at Sprawl-mart is autocrappy.*

arachnijig (ə-răk-nĭ'jĭg)

(n.) The involuntary dancing motion one makes when one accidentally walks into a spider web, or is told there's a spider on them.

automagically (ô'tə-măj'ĭ'kăl-lē)

(adv.) Automatically by a process that one does not understand or cannot be bothered to explain to anyone else.

Example: *Alex automagically fixed Sandra's computer.*

awesomnity (ô'səm'nĭ-tē)

(n.) The quantity or condition of being awesome.

Example: *The awesomnity of the giant banana split you made us is beyond measurement!*

B

baboon (bă-bün)

(n.) Possibly the highest state of being drunk one can achieve.

Example: *Dang man, you're a full-out baboon*!

Origin: Originating from the idea that one can go ape-crazy when one's behavior is uninhibited.

backronym (băk'rə-nĭm')

(n.) An acronym that was clearly thought of before the (usually dull-minded) phrase was crafted to fit it.

Example: *Determined Involved Supermodels Helping to End Suffering: DISHES!*

Note: The word *backronym* in no way connotes that the cause of the acronym is trivial, but merely serves to point out that the initials came before the phrase.

bacne (băk'nē)

(n.) acne of the back.

bactor (băk-tər)

(pron.) A bad actor.

Also: *bactress*

bagerno (băj'ûr-nō)

(n.) To get really, really stoned. This word only makes sense in that state of mind.

Example: *Dude, let's go bagerno.*

bambombatong (băm-bŏm-bə'tông)

(n.) Some form of an ape. A useful word to impress your kids at the zoo.

Origin: Names of several subspecies of apes combined into a single, all-inclusive name.

banana hammock (băn-ăn'ə hăm'ək)

(n.) A Speedo bathing suit or bikini briefs.

Origin: Mentioned on the popular sitcom, "Friends." However, there are possible earlier origins.

bandpulliphobia (bănd-pu'lə-fō'bē-ə)

(n.) The fear of pulling off a band-aid, especially when counting down from three.

banomaly (bənôm'ə-lē)

(n.) (fictitious) A banana free of bruises or other gross marks.

2. (n.) Any specific bruise found on a banana.

bananosecond (bə-năn'ə-sĕk'ənd)
   (n.) The time elapsed between slipping on a banana peel
   and hitting the ground.

barbit (bär-bĭt)
   (n.) A loose hair clinging to the face after a shave.

   Example: *After Bob shaved his beard, there was still a barbit*
   hanging to his chin that washed off when he took a shower.

barp (bärp)
   (v.) To burp and vomit simultaneously.

beautabulous (byü-tăb'yü'ləs)

(adj.) A word used to describe something that is both fabulous and beautiful.

Example: *The starry sky tonight is beautabulous!*

beautimus (byü'tə-məs)

(adj.) Something that is both beautiful and fabulous. Often used to describe something that worked out perfectly or in one's favor.

Example: *Beautimus! That catch was beautimus!*

Origin: An alternate combination of the words *beautiful* and *fabulous*.

becusing (bē-kyü-sĭng)

(adj.) Bemusing and confusing.

Example: *Your son is sticking carrots up his nose and then eating them. Very becusing!*

beebeesh (bē'bēsh)

(n.) A boo-boo, a child's injury, particularly one that can clearly be seen later, such as a bruise, scab, scratch, etc.

Origin: Coined in the mid-1960s by a 3-year-old.

beepilepsy (bēp'ə-lĕp'sē)

(n.) The seizure suffered in the process of finding and turning off a beeper, especially one that vibrates.

Example: *Dad had a beepilepsy while he was driving us home, and nearly ran off the road.*

beer goggles (bîr gŏg'əls)

(n.) A condition afflicting inebriated individuals, allowing mutual attraction between those who would ordinarily not be attracted.

See also: *beersightedness*

beer thirty (bîr thûr'tē)

(n.) Any time on the half hour that one decides to open and drink a beer.

beersightedness (bîr'sī'tĭd'nĭs)

(n.) The eye condition developed after "last call" in the bar which makes members of the opposite sex more attractive than they were three hours earlier.

See also: *beer goggles*

behunkis (bē-hŭng'kĭs)

(n.) Someone's bottom, behind, posterior. This term is strictly used to jest about a person's behind or to tell him or her to get moving.

Example: *You had better move that behunkis and get to school!*

belly twister (bĕl'ē twĭs'tər)

(n.) A plastic coated wire used to close a bag of bread or other twist-close item.

Origin: Possibly coined when someone was twisting a wire-tie at belly-button level, or because the tie resembles a belt which is tied around the waistline.

bendectomy (bĕnd'ĕk-tə'mē)

(n.) The procedure of bending something, usually metal, so that it fits properly where it was intended to fit.

Example: *We had to give the pipe a little bendootomy but then everything went together just fine.*

benefficient (bĕn'ə-fĭsh'ənt)

(adj.) When one thing or entity efficiently benefits another. Measured by the degree of efficiency of one thing or entity benefiting another.

benefriend (bĕn'ə-frĕnd)

(n.) A so-called friend with whom one partakes in activities not normally associated with mere friendship, often stereotyped as sexual acts, without fear of ruining the friendship and without any commitment. A friend with benefits.

besmirchify (bē-smûrch-ĭ-fī')

(v.tr.) Charge falsely or with malicious intent; attack the good name and reputation of someone.

Origin: As used by Don King.

bevamirage (bĕv'ə-mĭ-räzh')

(n.) The two or three inches of dark plastic on the bottom of a nearly empty two-liter cola bottle that fools the owner into thinking that there is at least one whole glass of soda remaining.

beveragitation (běv'răj'ĭ-tā'shən)

(n.) The disturbing feeling of loss and bewilderment one experiences when looking into an empty cup or mug that one was sure contained at least another mouthful.

Origin: A combination of *beverage* and *agitation*.

bifocalitis (bî-fô'kə-lī'tĭs)

(n.) A condition that afflicts wearers of bifocals that causes them to think they are reading a line of text or row of data straight across, when in actuality they are seeing a different line or row or a combination of different lines or rows. This often results in a mismatch between intent, information, and/or action.

bitsing (bĭt-sĭng)

(v.) The act of singing only small portions of songs, usually repeatedly. Variations include *bithum* and *bitspeak*.

Example: *If you are going to bitsing, at least get the words right!*

blaccent (blăk-cənt)

(n.) A manner of speaking in which one sounds like an African-American from "da hood."

blade runner (blād rŭn'ər)

(n.) The tendency of a ceiling fan to keep going five minutes after one has turned it off.

blamestorming (blām'stôr'mǐng)

(v.) A method of collectively finding one to blame for a mistake no one is willing to confess to. Often occurs in the form of a meeting of colleagues at work, gathered to decide who is to blame for a screw up.

Example: *OK guys, I'm not taking the fall for that screwed up order. Let's do a little blamestorming and decide who we can pin it on.*

blasphometer (blăs'fə-mē'tər)

(n.) A meter used to measure how blasphemous a just-uttered statement was. It is generally created by holding one's arms in front of oneself with elbows bent at right angles so that the left hand rests on top of the right elbow, and the right hand is directly below the left elbow. The left hand is then raised in an arc, like the needle on a speedometer, to indicate the severity of the blasphemy just uttered.

bleater (blē'tər)

(n.) A person who complains excessively when in a difficult situation, often disturbing others who are attempting to resolve the issue.

Origin: From *bleat*, to talk whiningly.

Example: *If that bleater would just shut up, I could figure out which way we're supposed to go.*

blend (blĕnd)

(n.) A friend made through mutual adoration of each other's blogs.

bligeck (blə-gĕk)

(interj.) An expression of disgust.

Origin: From the increasingly common term, *bleh*, meaning gross, and from either *geck*, to jeer, or from an onomatopoetic expression for a gag reflex.

blimple (blĭm'pəl)

(n.) A large pimple.

Origin: From *blimp*, a slang term for obesity, and *pimple*.

See also: *plumple*

blimpliments (blĭm'plə-mənts)

(n.pl.) High-calorie or high-fat toppings one adds to a low-calorie or low-fat food that effectively cancel out all the benefits of eating the healthy food in the first place.

blinknesia (blĭngk-knē'zhə)

(n.) When someone leaves her blinker on for a while after she has turned.

Origin: The contraction of *blink* and *amnesia*, partial or total loss of memory.

blong (blông)

(n.) An inordinately large and shiny piece of jewelry.

Example: *"Check out my blong, man!" "Whoa man, that's somethin' ginormous."*

Origin: A superlative of the slang term *bling*. A blending of *bling* and *bloated*.

blurple (blûr'pəl)

(n.) A color described as a mix between blue and purple.

bolognah (bəl-ō'nä)

(n.) The act of reaching for the bologna in the fridge but discovering that it is sticky and old.

Example: *He was hungry, but one look in the fridge and balognah struck him, and his quest for food continued.*

Origin: From *bologna* and *nah*, no.

boondongle (bün-dôn'gəl)

(n.) An unnecessary or wasteful peripheral device.

Example: *That USB-powered back massager is a boondongle.*

Origin: A blending of *boondocks*, a rural area, and *dongle*, a commonly used term for a serial connection.

borgasm (bôr-găz'əm)

(n.) A faked zenith of sexual excitement.

Example: *Yeah, I told Frank I had fun last night, but to tell you the truth, it was 100 percent borgasm.*

bovacious (bō'vā'shĕs)

(adj.) Of or pertaining to a cow; having cow-like characteristics.

Example: *Yes, it's like your hair is kind of bovacious.*

2. (adj.) Dull or boring; the life of a cow.

bowbaktry (bŏw'băk-trē)

(n.) The practice of bowing just to make the person one is facing bow back. A practice often taken advantage of in Asian countries.

See also: *salbaktry*

boything (boi-thĭng)

(n.) One of the male gender who believes he is a female's boyfriend, when in fact he is utterly despised by said female.

Example: *Claire, where's your creepy boything?*

See also: *not-boyfriend*

brain cloud (brān kloud)

(n.) A condition of the brain in which one forgets large amounts of information for a short period of time, often occurring when one is queried about small amounts of information.

See also: *cranial flatulation, brain fart, brain cramp.*

brain cramp (brān krămp)

(n.) The inability to get some information or action to occur because your brain is failing to come up with the correct action or response.

2. (n.) The polite version of brain fart or cranial flatulation.

Example: *Man, I knew the answer to the prof's question, but I had a major brain cramp!*

See also: *brain fart, cranial flatulation, brain cloud*

brain fart (brān färt)

(n.) Malfunction of the brain on a given thought process, usually occurring during an important situation.

See also: *cranial flatulation, brain cloud, brain cramp*

2. (n.) What one claims to have happened when failing to answer a simple question. Unlike a normal fart, these leave no revolting odor or any clue to their presence.

Example: *Bob: "What day of the week is it today, Fred?" Fred: "It's chili day in the cafeteria!" Bob: "No!... I asked what day of the week!" Fred: "Oh, brain fart... It's Friday."*

bridezilla (brīd-zĭl'ə)

(n.) A bride in the months prior to her wedding. Typically, these brides-to-be are spotted "coming out of the ocean" and "terrorizing Tokyo."

Example: *If you were in the bridal party, you'd know just what an encounter with bridezilla is like. The rest of the world just better take cover.*

briefently (brē'fənt-lē)

(adv.) Recently and for a very short period of time.

Example: *Have you seen Bob? Yes, he was here briefently.*

brinner (brĭn'ər)

(n.) A meal eaten between dinner and breakfast, sometimes known as a midnight feast.

bugly (bŭg'lē)

(adj.) Literally butt ugly. Beyond simply being ugly.

bumper sticker (bŭm'pər stĭk'ər)

(n.) A tattoo on one's lower back. More often a procedure that women have done. This term is used because, just like traditional bumper stickers, they provide something to read or look at while one is standing behind the wearer.

Example: *Honest, honey, I wasn't staring at her butt. I was just checking out her bumper sticker.*

bung (bŭng)

(v.) Banged; The past tense of bang.

Example: *Jimmy bung on the drums until his mother yelled at him for making such a ruckus.*

Bushify (büsh'ə-fī)

(v.tr.) To get something very wrong, in any area of life.

Example: *Seems that you've Bushified that one, Prime Minister.*

Bushism (büsh'ĭz'əm)

(n.) The combining of words into an unword that displays the user's attempt at verbal prowess.

Example: *A sample Bushism: After a hard day of "applicating" for jobs, I am still unemployed.*

Origin: A term coined to categorize all of President Bush's eccentric speech.

See also: *applicating*

bust (bŭst)

(v.) The act of hugging someone of a significant height difference, resulting in the shorter person's head getting crushed to the chest of the taller person.

Example: *"Sally busted me when I tried to give her a hug; she was nearly a foot taller than me."*

bustacate (bŭs'tä-kāt')

(v.) To wreck or destroy beyond repair.

C

caffeinatic (kă'fē'năt'ĭk)

(n.) Someone who is a fanatic about caffeine consumption.

caffiend (kă'fēnd)

(n.) One who is obsessed with consuming caffeine. Often surpasses caffeinatics in quantities of caffeine in the blood stream and in level of addiction.

calbliterate (kăl-blĭt'ə-rāt')

(v.tr.) To toy with something until it no longer works or is much worse than it originally was.

Example: *No, Sam didn't fix the TV. He futzed around with all the wires until he calbliterated it!*

Origin: From *calibrate*, to adjust to a standard, and *obliterate*, to erase or leave no trace.

calorosity (kăl'ə-rŏs'ĭ-tē)

(n.) A desire while dieting to see the dessert menu while still possessing the willpower to not order dessert.

Origin: From *calorie* and *curiosity*.

camouflush (kăm'ə-flŭsh)

(n.) The unnecessary flushing of a public restroom toilet to mask embarrassing bodily sounds.

Example: *I always make sure I camouflush before I go if my boss is in the restroom, too.*

capapult (kăp'ə-pŭlt')

(v.) The act of flinging one's hat or cap into the air, usually at the end of a graduation or when a large crowd is cheering.

cappus lockus (kăp'pəs lŏk'əs)

(n.) A dreaded affliction that causes one's cap lock to come on without his knowledge, causing people in a chatroom to think he is yelling at them for some time before he realizes his cap lock is on.

Example: *NO, I'M NOT MAD AT YOU! WHY DO YOU THINK THAT???!!!*

Carpal Thumal Syndrome (kär'pəl thŭm'əl sĭn'-drōm')

(n.) A condition of the thumbs that is brought on by the excessive use of a Blackberry or other similar device.

Origin: A variation on *carpal tunnel syndrome*.

cashamed (kə-shāmd')

(adj.) Feeling guilty or embarrassed about the amount of money one has.

catastrotree (kăt-ăs'trə-trē)

(n.) When a cat or kitten knocks over or pulls down a Christmas tree.

Example: *My cat, Jewel, caused a huge catastrotree.*

Origin: The blending of *cat*, *catastrophe*, and *tree,* suggesting a situation involving all three of these factors.

catjam (kăt-jăm)

(n.) A situation in which one or more pet cats are blocked from moving to another location because they don't want to pass too closely to each other.

Example: *A catjam occurred when Sylvester didn't have enough room to pass Tommy in the hallway.*

caukern (kô-kûrn)

(n.) A popcorn kernel that is stuck in one's teeth.

Origin: From *cauk*, a variant of *caulk,* a sealing material used to make things watertight, and *kern*, a shortened form of *kernel*.

Cell-Hell (sĕl-hĕl)

(n.) The place where a cell phone turns one's calls off due to bad reception. Such places include tunnels, overpasses, and the McDonald's drive-thru.

cellapse (sĕl-lăps')

(n.) A period of time when there is no cellphone reception.

Origin: A blending of *elapse*, *collapse*, and *cellphone*.

chairy (châr'ē)

(adj.) Describing someone who likes to chair in meetings, to preside, to be a master of ceremonies.

Examples: *Jimmy is every bit as chairy as Andrew, which spells trouble at a small institution like ours.*

She is a wonderful person, but maybe just a touch too chairy to share a household.

chaortic (kā-ôr'tĭk)

(adj.) A situation that is both orderly and chaotic.

chewsome (chü'səm)

(adj.) Attractively chewy.

Origin: Much like *toothsome*, only in relation to how chewable something is.

2. (adj.) Of a chewy texture.

3. (adj.) Very pleasant, pleasing, or exciting but with more texture.

Example: *Brian was given a chewsome offer.*

chicken-thirty (chĭk'ən-thûr'tē)

(n.) Refers to a ridiculously early time in the morning when the roosters start to crow.

Example: *I'd better stop drinking and go home. I have to be up at chicken-thirty.*

chillax (chĭ-lăks')

(v.) To chill and relax.

Example: *Just chillax, and I'll be right with you.*

Origin: Known to be used by a large number of people in Toronto, Canada and surrounding regions.

chipple (chĭp'əl)

(n.) Residue left on one's hands and clothes after eating a bag of chips.

Origin: From *chip* and *rubble*, a mass of angular fragments crumbled by natural or human forces.

chlorospud (klôr'ə-spŭd)

(n.) The substance that gives some potato chips their inexplicably green color. Many snackers have been tricked into thinking these green chips are a toy surprise.

Origin: From *chlorophyll*, a substance that gives plants their green color, and *spud*, a potato.

chopchopski (chŏp-chŏp'skē)

(adv.) Requesting someone move out of one's way.

Example: *Hey, you! Chopchopski!*

Origin: A Polish rendition on the phrase *chop chop*, meaning hurry up.

Chreaster (krē'stər)

(n.) A person who attends her place of worship only on major holidays, such as Christmas and Easter.

Example: *The Chreasters are coming! The church will be jammed!*

Chriskwanzakuh (krĭs'kwän'zə'kə)

(n.) The joint celebration of Christmas, Hanukkah, and Kwanzaa. Saying "Happy Chriskwanzakuh!" combines all three major holiday wishes into one big holiday wish.

circumvaculate (sûr'kəm-văk'yü-lāt)

(v.) To remain stationary while vacuuming in a circle around oneself.

clapperphobia (klăp'ər-fō-bē-ə)

(n.) An abnormal fear of clapping one's hands at concerts, events, or other gatherings when around a large number of people. Often attributed to the fear of drawing attention by a potentially loud clap.

claustropedic (klô'strə-pē'dĭk)

(adj.) A syndrome where the sufferer can't wear closed-toe footwear, even when it's needed. Mostly seen in the evenings during the winter.

Example: *This winter storm is dreadful, but the strappy sandals worn by the women in line at the nightclub prove how claustropedic they are.*

cleanaholic (klēn'ə-hôl'ĭk)

(n.) Someone who, in seeing a crumb on the floor, cleans the whole house again.

cleaverage (klēv'ər-ĭj)

(n.) The advantage women have over men when wearing a low-cut top.

clicklexia (klĭk-lĕk'sē-ə)

(n.) A computer-related disorder in which one has a tendency to double-click on items which only require one click, often resulting in two items opening instead of just one. This disorder is more often found in novices and aged computer users.

clicklinger (klĭk'lĭng'ər)

(n.) Anyone who holds the mouse button down, instead of just clicking it, in hopes that it will give the computer time to realize something has been selected.

clickulate (klĭk'yü-lāt')

(v.) Repetitive and nervous clicking of the mouse in a fervent attempt at making a webpage load faster.

clingons (klĭng-ŏnz)

(n.pl.) Little pieces of toilet paper that get stuck in one's behind, or to one's shoe.

clonedead (klōn-dĕd)

(adj.) A written document that has been copied until it is practically illegible and is therefore useless.

Example: *I received a copy of a scanned copy of a fax of a printout of a mimeographed copy of a fax of a copy, and it certainly was clonedead.*

coffeecan (kô'fē-kǎn)

(n.) A crumby car that has a loud exhaust. Often one will find ground rust particles falling off of the vehicle.

comatext (cō'mə-tĕkst)

(n.) Text that pleases the person who wrote it, but puts the reader into a coma.

comatoasty (kō'mə-tō'stē)

(adj.) Describing someone in a lethargic or unconscious state of mind brought on by an large amounts of warmth. Often, this state is intensified by the use of blankets or a large fire.

comedicide (kə-mē'dĭ-sīd')

(n.) The telling of a terrible joke that incorporates elements of a recently told good joke.

2. (n.) The retelling of a good joke, where the comedy of the joke is completely lost in the retelling.

3. (n.) The repetition of a comedic line, situation, or word until it has lost all meaning or humor.

comfordable (kŭm-fôr'də-bəl)

(adj.) That which is not only affordable but comfy as well.

commucapitalist (kŏm'yə-kăp'ĭ-tl-ĭst)

(n.) A political affiliation that crosses between a communist and a capitalist ideal. It is often used in describing the current state of Chinese society.

compulsive away disorder (kəm-pŭl'sĭv ə-wā' dĭs-ôr'dər)

(n.) A deficiency affecting those obsessed with constantly reading away messages on one's favorite instant messenger service.

compulsive slowpokyist (kəm-pŭl'sĭv slō'pōk'ē-ist)
(n.) Any person who, while driving or walking, perhaps on a highway or in a mall, hurries up to get in front of others, but then travels really slowly.

conaster (kə-năs'tər)
(n.) Antonym to disaster. The fortunate outcome of an almost imminent disaster; the sensation of a catastrophe narrowly averted and later remembered from the vantage point of safety.

Example: *There were several conasters in my life that I cannot recall without thanking God for his mercy.*

Origin: From Latin *cum*, with, and Greek *astron*, star.

condimentize (kŏn'də-mən-tīz')
(v.) The act of applying any form of condiment to a food product.

confirmative (kən-fûr'mə-tĭv)
(adj.) Describing a meeting or other action used to affirm one's confirmation.

Example: *That was certainly the longest, confirmative, company-wide meeting I have ever attended. All we did was make sure everyone was prepared for Friday's meeting.*

conflustered (kən-flŭs'tərd')
(adj.) Describing a situation in which one is so confused that he gets flustered.

Example: *My mother got me so conflustered while we were driving that I nearly put the car in the ditch.*

confuzzled (kən-fŭz'əld')

(adj.) Being both confused and puzzled; clueless or unclear.

Example: *Well, I have to admit I'm confuzzled by your grades. I've never had such a promising student do so poorly on exams.*

Origin: From *confused*, *fuzz*, and *puzzled*.

Note: Synonym of *confused*; antonym of *clear*.

contradick (kŏn'trə-dĭk)

(n) One who contradicts another primarily to make that person look foolish, unwise, uncool, or otherwise bad.

Example: *Yeah, I was wrong, but you don't have to be such a contradick about it.*

convercide (kŏn-vər-sīd)

(n.) The act of killing a conversation with a terrible comment.

Example: *Jacob: "I tell you the art of Van Gogh is truly timeless." Bradley: "Indeed I must say, old chap." Edgar: "I think I have a few head lice." Jacob: "A truly pleasant way to commit convercide, Edgar."*

conversate (kən-vûr'sāt)

(v.) To make conversation. An uncommon phrase used to make others believe one is smarter than one truly is.

Example: *Excuse us while we escape to the vestibule and conversate for a short time.*

corporashun (kôr'pə-rā'shŭn)

(n.) Any variation on a company or product name created with the intent to mock or shun it.

Example: *Some corporashuns include: Internet Exploder by Microshaft, Home Cheap-o, Northworst Airlines.*

cowversation (kău'vər-sā'shən)

(n.) A topic people continue to milk over and over because they've run out of other things to say.

Example: *"Great weather we're having. Just can't get over how sunny it is." "Yeah..." "So, it's not too hot, just bright. I love that."*

crackerslacker (krăk'ər-slăk'ər)

(n.) The crackers that are found under the aluminum or plastic pouch when one finishes a package.

cranial flatulation (krā'nē-əl flăch'yə'lā'shən)

(n.) Condition of the brain to cease functioning mid-sentence, frequently occurring during important meetings where one must impress others, leaving the user of said brain with a blank stare.

See also: *brain fart, brain cloud, brain cramp*

crispinization (krĭs'pĭ'nĭ-zā'shən)

(n.) The process that is undergone when a perfectly gooey, fresh baked chocolate chip cookie is left out for a day and a half, rendering it inedible and suitable for brickwork.

cromulent (crôm-yü-lənt)

(adj.) Being well-formed; legitimate; of a word, especially a neologism, that is not previously attested in the language but obeys its rules of word-formation.

Origin: This word was originally coined in season 3, episode 13 of The Simpsons TV series in 1996.

crubbers (crŭb'ərs)

(n.pl.) Little rubber things that appear after one uses a pencil eraser.

crudmuffin (krŭd-mŭf'ĭn)

(n.) An item of food so disgusting that one can't even stomach it.

2. (n.) A food so sick-looking that one can't tell what it's supposed to be.

Example: *I think the cafeteria is serving crudmuffins again.*

crustmonger (krŭst-mŏng'gər)

(n.) A person who is extremely crusty.

Origin: From *crusty*, rude and ill-mannered, and *monger*, to deal in the market of.

cryiest (krī'ē'əst)

(adj.) Describing something or someone who has made one cry more than anything or anyone else ever has before.

Example: *The cryiest moment of my life was the day our cat Butterball died.*

cuspular (kŭsp-û'ler)

(adj.) The act of being on the edge between two extremes.

Example: *There appear to be a lot of people with cuspular sexuality.*

Origin: From *cusp*, the pointed end of, and *-ular,* of or relating to.

cutlerimmunodeficiency (kŭt'lər-ĭm'yə-nō-dĭ-fĭsh'ən-sē)

(n.) An innate, acquired, or induced inability to pick the right piece of cutlery out of the silverware drawer.

D

dallywaddle (dăl'ē-wŏd'l)

(v.) To take an excessively long time, especially involving motion on foot; to dilly-dally in going somewhere; to drag one's feet.

Example: *Sara is a born dallywaddler — there's always "one more thing" she has to check before we can leave the house.*

Origin: From *dilly-dally*, to waste time, and *waddle*, to walk in short steps and sway back and forth.

dark matter song (därk măt'ər sŏng)

(n.) A song of such awfulness that it alone outweighs the rest of an artist's or band's body of work.

Example: *"Shiny Happy People" is REM's dark matter song and "Walk of Life" is Dire Straits'.*

deadvertise (dĕd'vər-tīz')

(v.tr.) To advertise and promote political causes by death.

Example: *Terrorism is nothing but the art of deadvertising.*

Origin: The combination of *dead* and *advertise*.

decidribel (dĕs'ə-drĭ'bəl)

(n.) A unit used to measure the stupidity of a speech.

See also: *dribel*

decompliment (dē'kŏm'plə-mənt)

(v.) To immediately insult someone after complimenting them, thereby rendering the compliment void.

defriend [somebody] (dĭ-frĕnd')

(v.tr.) To break off friendly relations with somebody; antonym to befriend.

Example: *He defriended me a year after we met, with no reason or explanation. He just stopped calling, period.*

déjà foo (dā'zhä fü)

(n.) A mistake one has already seen or made once before.

Example: *Did we really elect Bush twice? It was déjà foo.*

déjà fu (dā'zhä fü')

(n.) The illusion of having already been kicked in a certain way before.

Origin: From *déjà vu* and *kung fu*.

déjà view (dā-zhä vyü)

(n.) A phenomenon that occurs after one watches a television show for the first time, then doesn't watch it again for a while, then sees it again and the station happens to be re-airing the one episode the person already saw.

delayed billelation (dĭ-lād bĭ'lə-lā'shən)

(v.) Any usable denomination of money, found in the pockets of a coat, jacket, or pair of pants that has been put away for a long period of time, which creates a long-lasting joyous feeling of satisfaction once found.

Example: *"Why are you so happy today?" "I suppose I'm still delay billelated about the ten bucks I found in my winter coat from last year."*

dementocracy (dĭ-měn'tŏk'rə-sē)

(n.) A society in which the most demented members rise to the top.

dentarded (děn'tärd'ĕd)

(adj.) People who refuse, are afraid of, or simply ignore dental visits.

depocket (dē-pŏk'ĭt)

(n.) To fall from a pocket due to one becoming horizontal.

Example: *Dude, your change is depocketing! Catch it!*

2. (n.) The act of unloading the contents of one's pockets before lying or sitting on a bed or couch. Especially done by males; items are usually deposited into their hat, or, in the event of staying the night, into their shoes.

destructinate (dĭ-strŭk'tə-nāt')

(v.tr.) The act of destroying something entirely, leaving nothing but atomic particles.

Example: *I am going to destructinate you!*

desuckify (dē-sŭk'ə-fī)

(v.tr.) To ameliorate one's situation, work, idea, item, place; to make less disagreeable.

Example: *Having that new hottie working in the mailroom really desuckifies the place.*

detrivenient (dĕt'rə-vēn'yənt)

(adj.) Being convenient to the point of detriment.

Example: *Living next door to a liquor store can be very detrivenient.*

dialup (dī'əl-ŭp')

(adj.) Something that is very slow.

Example: *We missed the first five minutes of the movie because our waiter went dialup with the check!*

Origin: From slow dial-up modem internet connections.

dietribe (dī'ə-trīb')

(n.) An irate sermon or lecture on healthy eating.

differentiality (dĭf'ə-rĕn'shē-ăl'ĭ-tē)

(n.) The practice of being different.

Example: *Alexandria welcomed differentiality.*

digiocrity (dĭ'jē-ŏk'rĭ-tē)

(n.) The culture of replacing high-quality analog systems with lower-quality but more convenient digital systems.

Example: *The rapid replacement of film cameras with digital is a true sign of digiocrity.*

dignitude (dĭg'nə-tüd')

(n.) A dignified attitude.

dinch (dĭnch)

(n.) A meal eaten between lunch and dinner. The compliment to brunch. One of two meals eaten by those on a two-meal-a-day diet.

Origin: A contraction of *dinner* and *lunch*.

dingy (dĭng-ē)

(v.tr.) To ignore someone or something deliberately.

Example: *"I tried to phone her, but she dingied me."*

Origin: Likely from the tendency of a *dingy*, a small boat, to be ignored in a shipyard.

dirty bin (thə dûr'tē bĭn)

(n.) A large bin of discount products, such as unwanted toys or DVDs, that can be found at large supermarkets.

disasterbacle (dĭ-zăs'tər-băk'əl)

(n.) An event or procedure that has gone terribly wrong.

Example: *The Pistons versus Pacers game turned into a disasterbacle.*

disconfusing (dĭs'kən-fyüz'ĭng)

(adj.) Very, very confusing.

discorsage (dĭs'kôr-säzh')

(v.) Removal of a corsage.

discrimihate (dĭ-skrĭm'ə-hāt'')

(v.) To hate someone for being different.

Example: *"Dis foo be straight discrimihatin' on a playa. I'm just tryin' to gets mine."*

disemvowel (dĭs'ĕm-văü'əl)

(v.) T rmv ll th vwls frm spm r thr dslkd txt. Translation: To remove all the vowels from spam or other disliked text.

Origin: From *disembowel*, remove the insides of, and *vowel*.

disgreenimation (dĭs-grēn'ə-mā'shən)

(n.) Requiring meticulous analysis to verify the environmental credentials of "green" products or services, while not applying the same level of rigor in assessing the environmental impact of all other products or services.

Origin: From *discrimination* and *green*, signifying environmentally friendly.

2. (n.) Expecting green technologies to compete on an uneven playing field.

Example: *I sense a bit of disgreenimation in that infrastructure for electricity from conventional sources was funded by the state via the tax system, while solar photovoltaic hot water systems are installed at the expense* *of householders who choose to install them, only sometimes with partial subsidy.*

3. (n.) Using economic or social arguments in isolation to justify a particular action which has a range of negative environmental consequences.

Example: *Senator John Doe expressed extreme disgreenimation when he told voters that, "Building this gas-powered plastic refinery plant creates jobs and earns export revenue."*

dishwater dysentery (dĭsh'wȯt'ər dĭs'ən-tĕr'ē)
(n.) An escape from doing chores, in which one finds oneself suddenly having to use the bathroom upon realizing or being told that it is his or her turn to clean up after dinner, specifically in reference to washing the dishes.

Example: *Hmm, that's odd. Jack and Mike both had to go to the bathroom the second I asked for help in the kitchen. I think a bad epidemic of dishwater dysentery is hitting our apartment!*

Origin: From *dishwater* and *dysentery*, an intestinal disorder plagued by diarrhea.

disluminate (dĭs-lü'mə-nāt')
(v.) To take light away from something.

Example: *With a flick of the switch the room was disluminated.*

disorientation (dĭs-'ôr'ē-ĕn-tā'shən)

(n.) A gathering in which attendees leave more confused than when they arrived.

2. (n.) Confusing introductory instruction concerning a new situation.

Example: *Well, that meeting about the new accounting system was a real disorientation.*

disremember (dĭs'rĭ-məm'bər)

(v.) To remember something incorrectly.

Example: *I disremembered what time it happened; I told you it happened at 2 p.m., but it really happened at 12 a.m.*

distashion (dĭs-tăsh'ən)

(n.) Someone's poor fashion sense.

Example: *She was wearing a pink top and a red skirt — it was such a distashion!*

Origin: From *disaster* or *distaste* and *fashion*.

dject (dē-jĕkt)

(v.) The overwhelming urge of a music connoisseur to wait until the end of the currently playing song before changing the song or ejecting the compact disc.

Example: *Just wait for a moment while I dject this CD and put on something else.*

Origin: From the term *DJ*, disc jockey, and *eject*.

docuphobia (dŏc'ū-fō'bē-ə)

(n.) The fear of using documentation, usually resulting from a previous traumatic event, such as programming a VCR.

dogelation (dŏg'ē-lāʹshən)

(n.) The ridiculously enthusiastic joy with which one's canine friend greets one at the door, expressed by tail wagging, running in circles, spreading dog germs across one's face with its tongue, and the like.

Origin: From *doggy* and *elation*.

donk (dŏngk)

> (v.) To speak in a pompous and circuitous manner,
> inventing words, and adding meaningless prefixes and
> suffixes to existing words.

> **Origin:** Back formation of the continuous tense, *donking*,
> from boxing promoter Don King.

> 2. (v.) To smack (one's head) in a dumbfounded manner.

> **Origin:** From *bonk*; the *d-* often comes from interjecting *duh*
> while bonking something.

doodeuce (dü-dyüs)

> (n.) Bodily waste removal of the second variety.

dostinate (dŭst'ə-nāt')

> (v.) To tell someone not to do something when one has not
> tried it oneself and does not know what it's like.

> **Example:** *Joe: "Don't study biomechanics." Tom: "Don't
> dostinate me! You've never studied biomechanics in your
> life!"*

> **Origin:** From *dost*, second person form of do, and possibly
> from *procrastinate*.

dotbomb (dŏt-bŏm)

> (n.) An internet venture doomed to failure.

> 2. (n.) A presentation where a doomed company is touted
> as a sure success.

> **See also:** *dotcomedy*

dotcomedy (dŏt-kŏm'ĭ-dē)

(n.) An internet venture that becomes a hilarious failure.

Origin: *Bill quit his big corporate job and went to work for a dotcom whose whole business was keeping track of URL expirations. He should've known it would become a dotcomedy.*

2. (n.) A presentation where a doomed company is touted as a sure success; sometimes followed by evil laughter coming from a competing company.

See also: *dotbomb*

dotcommie (dŏt-kŏm'ē)

(n.) Any ultra-liberal anti-American blogger.

dotcomword (dŏt-kŏm-wûrd)

(n.) Any word made up in an attempt to increase the rank of the term which it was made to describe, and to steal traffic from the websites to which it was submitted.

Example: *Dooderspoodle - The scoop used to clean up cat litter. See dooderspoodle.com for more information. (This is just an example dotcomword; dooderspoodle.com doesn't really exist ... yet.)*

downlifting (dăün-lĭft'ĭng)

(adj.) Describing something that causes depression. Opposite of uplifting; synonym of depressing.

Origin: *That movie was so downlifting that I just want to go home and curl up in bed.*

Dr. Pepsier (dŏk'tər pĕp'sē'ər)

(n.) The result of mixing Dr. Pepper and Pepsi.

drain salad (drān săl'əd)

(n.) The scrambled collection of various wet food scraps and chunks found in the drain stopper after washing the dishes.

Example: *Eww, who didn't clean out the sink? That drain salad is starting to stink.*

dramastic (drə-măs'tĭk)

(adj.) Dramatic and drastic.

dreadvertise (drĕd'vər-tīz')

(v.) To advertise by using dreadful tactics; to engage in military propaganda.

dremble (drĕm'bəl)

(v.) The action of a spider when it slowly descends on its web, especially a spider of the daddy longlegs order.

Origin: From *droop* and *tremble*.

dribel (drĭ'bəl)

(n.) A unit used to express relative difference in power or intensity between two stupid or childish speeches, often relating to drunken speech.

Example: *He's so drunk he must be talking at about 54 dribels! No wonder you can't understand him.*

Origin: From Old English *dreflian*, drivel, and *decibel*.

drunkword (drŭngk-wûrd)

(n.) Any unword that is submitted to an unword website by an inebriated person.

Example: *An excellent drunkword: Vanessott, meaning Vanessa is really hot.*

Origin: From all the really dumb words that we find being submitted late at night.

dudely (düd'lē)

(adv.) Descriptive of a woman with mannish or masculine qualities.

Example: *That chick is hot, but she has dudely hands.*

dudette (dü'dĕt')

(n.) A female dude.

Example: *Welcome dudes and dudettes!*

dumpfounded (dŭmp'fäünd'ĕd)

(adj.) The inability to locate a city dump that will accept a given sort of rubbish.

Example: *I'm trying to get rid of this used transmission fluid, but so far have been dumpfounded.*

dumpie (dŭmp'ē)

(acro.) A Downwardly-mobile, Under-employed, Middle-aged Professional.

Example: *We thought we were on top of the world when we worked for the broker, but we were all laid off last year, so now we're just a bunch of dumpies.*

dünken häcken (dŭng'kən hăk'ən)

(n.) Violent coughing attack brought on by inhaling the powdered sugar on a doughnut.

Example: *Dude, slow down when you're eating that doughnut. That dünken häcken is embarrassing.*

dunlop (dŭnlôp)

(v.) The action of a man's large, flabby stomach that is so huge it can no longer be contained by the pants but must flop over the top. Sometmes called *dunlop's disease*.

Example: *"Yo' belly dunlop over yo' belt!"*

Origin: From the words *done* and *flop*.

dyslection (dĭs-lĕk-shən)

(n.) An election stricken with a case of dyslexia, often referring to the infamous mix-up in the Presidential Election of 2000. One might say the Y2K bug actually happened in this case.

Example: *I hope those suspicious electronic voting machines don't give us another dyslection in 2008.*

E

e-touch (ē'tŭch)

(n.) A method of staying in contact with friends by e-mail or other electronic devices.

Example: *Hey, do you have my screen name so we can keep in e-touch?*

earp (ûrp)

(n.) To vomit.

Example: *I think I'm going to earp.*

Origin: Possibly an onomatopoeic word invented by someone who didn't quite get in a full sentence when he said he was going to vomit.

ebanatic (ē-bā-năt'ĭk)

(n.) An online bidder who bids relentlessly on an item until he wins without regard to the actual cost — almost always bidding more than retail.

Example: *My dad is such an ebanatic. He paid $200 on ebay for those new hubcaps, and I saw the exact same hubcaps at AutoMart for $125!*

Origin: The contraction of *lunatic* and the popular auction website *ebay*.

ediot (ē-bē-ət)

(n.) A person who, after giving someone material to edit, continues to revise that same material without telling the person he just gave it to.

edutainjugal (ĕj'ə-tân'jü-gəl)

(adj.) Salacious material presented on mass media as educational and consumed as entertainment by its audience.

Origin: From *educational*, *entertainment*, and *-jugal,* as in conjugal (Latin *juxta*, near).

EGGS (ĕgz)

(acro.) Electronically Generated Groups and Situations, such as smart mobs or *bookcrossing* groups, that use the web to foment their social bonds in real space and time.

Example: *Do you participate in any EGGS? - Yes, I am a seasoned EGG'er.*

emo (ē-mō)

(n.) Abbreviated from "emotive hardcore," relating to a genre of music featuring bands that use emotional and personal lyrics.

2. (adj.) An individual who is a follower of emo music.

Example: *You're so emo.*

3. (adj.) A style of dress used by followers of emo. This dress sense includes trucker caps, long fringes for boys, short hair for girls, black clothes, and tight trousers.

emongous (ĭ-mŏng'gəs)

(adj.) Something large, usually electronic.

Example: *Johny's new TV is emongous!*

Origin: Stems from combining *enormous* and *humongous*. The use of *e-* denotes a relation to electronics.

Emotional-Tourette's (ĭ-mō'shə-nəl tû-rəts')

(n.) An affliction in which one cannot control a need to announce how one feels to uninterested parties.

enclownter (ĕn-klăün'tər)

(n.) A brief, usually unpleasant, encounter with a clown.

Englishification (ĭng-glĭsh-ĭ-fĭkcāˈshən)
(n.) The alteration, while speaking a language other than English, of an English word to make it sound like a word in the language one is speaking, or attempting to speak.

Example: *Miruku is a Japanese Englishification of the word milk.*

enjoice (ĕn-joisˈ)
(v.tr.) Using false joy to talk someone into sharing an undesirable task; to entrap somebody by the appearance of joy, to deceive or trick into difficulty.

Example: *He looked extremely happy with his winning ticket, and he enjoiced me into entering these sweepstakes, which I would never have done otherwise.*

Origin: From *en-*, meaning surrounding something or somebody or placing it within something, and Old French *joie*, meaning joy and an expression of happiness.

enjoyful (ĕn-joiˈfəl)
(adj.) To be in a state of enjoyment; to find something joyful.

Example: *Wow, making up new words is really enjoyful!*

enterstainment (ĕnˈtər-stānˈmənt)
(n.) Dubious, dreadful entertainment which leaves one feeling stained.

Example: *The enterstainment value of that R-rated movie was quite high.*

excess bunnage (ĕk'sĕs bŭ'nĭj)

(n.) When one has more buns than hot dogs at a cook out, or when one's bun is too long for the hot dog. The opposite problem is called *excess frankage*.

evidentually (ĕv'ĭ-dĕn'chü-ə-lē)

(adv.) That according to the evidence available, sooner or later, a given event is bound to occur.

Example: *I saw the poster; evidentually REM is coming to the county fair.*

Origin: A combination of *evidently* and *eventually*.

ex (ĕks)

(v.) To render outdated, make obsolete, relegate to the past.

Example: *He exed his girlfriend and now feels lonely.*

Origin: From Latin *ex*, out of.

exaccurate (ĭg-zăk'yər-ĭt)

(adj.) Exactly accurate.

eyelidology (ī-lĭd-ŏl'ə-jē)

(n.) The study of one's own eyelids. Sometimes used as an excuse for sleeping in class.

Example: *That kid with his head on his desk at the back of the room is majoring in eyelidology.*

F

fabramblicate (făb-răm'blĭ-kăt)

(v.) The act of incessantly lying about "facts," until one forgets what one has previously lied about and contradicts oneself.

Origin: A blending of *fabricate* and *ramble*.

fabtastic (făb-tăs'tĭk)

(adj.) Describing anything that is both fabulous and fantastic.

fanaddict (făn'ə-dĭkt)

(n.) One who insists on sleeping with a fan on during cold weather while taking refuge under blankets.

2. (n.) A regular viewer of any celebrity news television syndication.

fantanation (făn'tənā'shən)

(n.) To have a very creative, mystical imagination.

Example: *You have a great fantanation.*

fartagogue (färt'ə-gŏg')

(n.) A place that most people find safe to pass gas. This place can often be identified by its horrid odor.

fartburn (färt'bûrn')

(n.) A condition caused by excessive farting.

Origin: From *fart* and *heartburn*.

faux-flatulance (fō-flăch'ə-ləns)

(n.) The fart-like noise a chair makes while moving or sitting on it, causing one's friends to accuse one of farting no matter how many times one says it was the chair.

fauxfile (fō-fīl)

(n.) A profile on any of the internet dating sites with alluring content detailing a non-existent person. Sometimes fauxfiles are created to elicit a response from a specific person.

Example: *I had a hunch my boyfriend was playing around on me. When he contacted my dating fauxfile, it confirmed it.*

federal (fĕd'ər-əl)

(adj.) Very real, or great; serious; official.

Example: *Yo, those chicken strips were federal!*

Origin: Derived from the use of *federal* in government terms. When something is raised to a federal level, it becomes more serious than if it were simply a state matter.

femail (fē-māl)

(n.) Nagging mail or email reminders.

femme du jour (fĕm də zhŏŏr)

(n.) Literally woman of the day; the latest girlfriend of a man who, after his divorce, has been unable or unwilling to maintain a long-term relationship.

Example: *Yeah, I met Bunny, Dad's femme du jour. Wanna bet on how long is this one's gonna last?*

fiblag (fĭb-lăg)

(n.) The period of time that elapses after a police officer asks a suspect a simple question, such as, "What is your last name?"

fibliography (fĭb'lē-ŏg'rə-fē)
> (n.) The sources one cites on a research paper for which one did no research at all.

fictionary (fĭk-shə-nĕr'ē)
> (n.) A fictitious dictionary.

fidiot (fĭd'ē-ət)
> (n.) A very foolish person. Not to be confused with *idiot*, a foolish person.

> **Origin:** Derived from the slang term *fugly* meaning very ugly, and from Latin *idiota* meaning an ignorant person.

filarious (fĭ-lâr'ē-əs)
> (adj.) Extremely funny; freaking hilarious.

FIMS (fĭms)
> (acro.) Foot-In-Mouth Syndrome.

> **Example:** *My boyfriend told my dad, who's a retired admiral, that military people are bores. What a bad case of the FIMS!*

finkler (fĭng'klər)
> (n.) A ragamuffin; a hooligan.

> **Example:** *My purse is missing! It must have been stolen by some finkler on the streets.*

firmth (fûrmth)
> (n.) The state or level of firmness of an object. Normally used when squeezing fruit or other semi-squishy objects.

fivehead (fīv'hĕd')

(n.) The body part commonly referred to as the forehead, only larger or higher due to a receding hairline or facial structure.

Example: *Check out the fivehead on that old man.*

Origin: From *fore-* in *forehead*, a homonym of the number four. Adding one makes this a *fivehead*.

flabbergusted (flăb'ər-gŭst'ĕd)

(adj.) To be shocked and astonished and disgusted all at the same time.

Example: *He bent over to fix the water pipe and I was so flabbergusted.*

Origin: The blending of *flabbergasted* and *disgusted*.

flaberjastic (flăb'ər-jăst'ĭk)

(interj.) A word used to express something good or fantastic. Commonly used when one can't think of a word to describe something. Often, nobody knows what it means, but its peculiar sound gives it away as meaning something good.

Example: *That breakfast was flaberjastic, Mrs. Smith!*

flake (flāk)

(n.) Slang. A knock-off production or product.

Example: *This grocer's brand orange juice is just a flake made from a powder mix.*

Flakespeare (flāk'spîr)

(n.) A person who thinks she is qualified to rewrite someone's work.

Example: *The Flakespeare's version of Little Women was lame compred to Louisa May Alcott's original.*

Origin: Clearly from famous writer *Shakespeare*. And from *flake*, referring to a knock-off production.

flashionable (flăsh'ə-nə-bəl)

(adj.) Being both flashy and fashionable.

flatcat (flăt-kăt)

(n.) A domesticated animal often seen in the middle of the road after many tires have driven over it. Generally, any miscellaneous or unknown type of road kill. Sometimes useful as a frisbee.

flatterful (flă'tər-fəl)

(adj.) To be full of flattery.

Example: *I'm glad you like my haircut. You're feeling rather flatterful today, I see.*

flavorite (flā'vər-ĭt)

(adj.) Referring to a flavor that is preferred above all others.

Example: *Peas are my most flavorite vegetable.*

flippoyance (flĭ-poi'əns)

(n.) The annoyance of hair that constantly needs to be flipped or shaken out of one's eyes.

Example: *Her hair's flippoyance finally drove her to the point of pulling it into a ponytail when she jogged.*

FLK (ĕf ĕl kă)

(acro.) Funny Looking Kid; common birth center term for a newborn who comes out looking "not quite right," but not so irregular as to be able to give him/her a label.

Example: *Baby Joan is an FLK.*

flugi (flü'gē)

(n.) A cross between phlegm and a lugi that can get caught at the back of one's throat, becoming nearly impossible to spit out or blow out of one's nose.

flustrate (flŭs'trāt)

(v.) To fluster and frustrate simultaneously.

fo (fō)

(prep.) Slang. For; because of.

Example: *"Fo real?" "Fo shizzle."*

Origin: Ghetto form of the word *for*.

focustrate (fō'kəs-trāt)

(v.) To both focus and concentrate, often achieving a higher level of focus and concentration than one achieves simply by focusing or concentrating.

foodgitive (füd-jĭ-tĭv)

(adj.) Any vegetable that sneaks over a partition of a TV dinner tray into either the main course or dessert area.

Example: *Call for backup! We have foodgitive beets in the chocolate pudding!*

foxymoron (fŏk'sē-môr'ŏn')

(n.) A member of the opposite sex blessed with beauty and cursed with stupidity, whose presence causes contradictory feelings of attraction and repulsion.

Example: *Yeah, Jenna has a great body, but the next time that foxymoron counts on her fingers, we're through.*

foyeurism (foi'ər-ĭzm)

(n.) An action born of curiosity in which the curious person lurks in the foyer for a family member to return from a date in hopes of spying on the good-night kiss; usually involving younger siblings and parents.

frafe (frāf)

(adj.) Fairly safe from danger, harm, or evil; only slightly more safe than unsafe.

Example: *You're safe here. Well, frafe anyway.*

frankquilized (frăng'kwə-līzd)

(v.tr.) When, by some fluke or alignment of planets, one has the same amount of hot dogs and hot dog buns. Also, when one's hot dog is the same length as its bun.

See also: *excess bunnage*

freaky deaky (frē'kē dē'kē)

(adj.) Wickedly weird.

Origin: An extreme form of *freaky*. From the common practice of making up a second word to rhyme with the first — both of which end in a ē sound, such as *gravy travy*.

fridiculous (frĭ-dĭk'yə-ləs)

(adj.) Beyond absurd; freaking ridiculous.

frienemy (frĕn'ə-mē)

(n.) A person who acts as though she is your friend so as to gain information for use against you.

Frito Laylien (frē'tō lā'lē-ən)

(n.) Any green potato chip believed to have traveled from a far off galaxy and invaded a bag of earthling potato chips. Occasionally found to travel in groups.

Origin: The blending of *alien* and snack giant *Frito-Lay*.

frogwash (frôg'wôsh')

(n.) Balderdash; ridiculous or valueless communication.

Origin: A more sonorous synonym of the more common *hogwash*.

frost butt (frôst bŭt)

(n.) The condition that snowboarders with baggy pants, or any low riders, suffer from when the temperature drops below freezing.

fryfugee (frī'fyü-jē')

(n.) A French fry found loose in the bottom of a fast food bag.

See also: *fugifry* and *stries*

fuelderment (fyü'əl'dər-mənt)

(n.) The confusion at an unfamiliar gas station over how to activate the gas pump.

Example: *Fuelderment fell upon Dharma as she tried to figure out whether to lift the handle and push the button or push the button and lift the handle.*

Origin: From *fuel* and *bewilderment*.

fugifry (fyü'jĭ-frī)

(n.) A French fry that has escaped from the smaller French fry sleeve into the larger takeout bag from a fast food burger joint. When the bag contains the components of several individuals' meals, fugifries are considered community property, though they are usually claimed by the person charged with passing out the food.

Origin: From *fugitive* and *French fry*.

See also: *fryfugee* and *stries*

fulfart (ful'färt)

(interj.) Full speed ahead.

Origin: A Norwegian phrase that has worked its way into the English language.

fundage (fŭn'dĭj)

(n.) Money; funds.

funnity (fŭn'ĭ-tē)

(n.) Great fun.

Example: *After the opening exercises, funnity ensued.*

Origin: A play on the term, *hilarity*, altered in relation to *fun*.

futility belt (fyü-tĭl'ĭ-tē bĕlt)

(n.) A belt, like that of a policeman, that has so many things attached to it that he or she can barely sit down.

Example: *I knew the cop was coming from the clanging of his futility belt.*

Origin: From *utility* and *futility*, frivolousness or uselessness.

fuzzies (fŭz'ēz)

(n.) The feeling of being in a dream during the day, as though one's eyes are clouded. Often occurs the day after a party night, or from lack of sleep. May also occur on a bright sun-shiny day in the form of *warm fuzzies*.

fuzzword (fŭz'wûrd')

(n.) A word, usually a buzzword, which has no precise meaning even in context.

G

gamovation (gă'mō-vâ-shən)

(n.) The tendency to swerve one's body back and forth while playing a game — usually involving car racing — on a TV game set.

Origin: From *game* and *move*.

gank (găngk)

(v.) To take for one's self; to steal a part of a song from another song and pretend it's one's own.

Example: *"You totally ganked that chord progression from Ace of Base."*

Origin: The union of *grab* and *yank*.

garbpaction (gärb-păk'shən)

(n.) The process of pushing garbage deeper down into a garbage can with one's foot.

Origin: The contraction of *garbage* and *compaction*.

garfu (gär-fü)

(n.) Stuff accidentally walked through that sticks to one's shoe.

Origin: From Old Italian, *garbo*, grace or clothing, and Old High German *fuotar*, food. The use of *-fu* suggests that food is the primary substance which sticks to one's shoe.

gaspopulater (găs-pŏp'yü-lāt'ər)

(n.) Gaseous expulsion, as a result of drinking soda pop, that does not come out until an hour or more later.

Origin: The blending of *gas*, *soda pop*, *populate*, and the phrase *smell you later*.

gastralcombustulate (găs'trəl-kəm-bŭst'yə-lāt')

(v.in.) To pass gas.

Origin: From *gastral*, relating to the stomach, and *combust*, to burn.

gear goggles (gîr gŏg'əls)

(n.) Thinking someone is more attractive than they really are because of the gear they are wearing. Especially in reference to ski or snowboard gear.

Origin: From *beer goggles,* in reference to equipment or gear.

geekening (gē'kən-ĭng)

(v.) The process of becoming a geek.

See also: *geekify*

geekify (gēk'ə-fī)

(v.) To turn someone to the geek side of the force — most often turning someone else into a geek through mentorship.

gendrofasten (jĕndrō'făsən)

(v.) When someone, normally a young child, refers to all people with one gender, whether it's accurate or not.

Example: *Alice gendrofastened when she called Grandpop "she."*

Origin: From *gender* and *fasten*, to hold firmly to.

2. (v.) The way small children use one word, often the only one they know in that category, to describe all matters of similar appearance.

Example: *A child is gendrofastened when he or she sees all things one drinks as being "juice," everything one uses to eat with are called "bowls," or every four-legged animal at the zoo is a "doggie."*

generiatrics (jə-nĕr'ē-āt'rĭks)

(n.) The behaviors and shopping habits of an elderly person who, due to living on a fixed income, can no longer afford to buy name-brand merchandise.

geshphincto (gĕsh-fĭng-tō)

(v.) Totally gone, destroyed, erased, or otherwise obliterated.

Example: *When I got back, the car was geshphincto, gone, vamoosed.*

Origin: Possibly a reference to being gone by way of expulsion from the body as in *sphincter*, but more likely made to sound like a foreign word, and thus express a level of sophistication.

ghastipate (găstə-pāt')
(v.) When a confused state of mind causes one's vocalization to become mixed-up, such that part of one's speech does not sound clear.

Example: *"Wai..I..nev...mean..t..hur..y..." "Are you ghastipated?"*

Origin: From *flabbergast* and *constipate*.

Gibbonism (gĭb'ən-ĭz-əm)
(n.) A word or phrase said, heard, or otherwise related to the character, Peter Gibbons, from the hit movie "Office Space." Such phrases lend themselves well to spice up otherwise dull or unproductive office meetings and can be used to mock the few co-workers who have not seen "Office Space."

gidiot (gĭd'ē-ət)
(n.) One who is giddy with love.

gihugic (jī-hyü'jĭk)
(adj.) A size descriptor indicating something bigger than huge.

Example: *That bass is gihugic.*

Origin: From *gigantic* and *huge*.

ginormous (jī-nôr′məs)

(adj.) Used to describe something so large that it is gigantic and enormous.

Example: *"Millicent, that 32-pound cat of yours is ginormous!" "That's freakin' huge! That's ginormous!"*

girlapse (gûr-lăps′)

(v.) The act in which a tomboy momentarily displays a feminine characteristic.

Origin: From *girl* and *relapse*.

gleak (glēk)

(n.) A fountain of saliva that spurts out of the mouth in large droplets.

Example: *When I opened my mouth to talk to him, I gleaked on his arm instead! Argh!*

2. (v.) When a person extends the muscles in his mouth in such a way as to send a minimal amount of watery saliva a great distance.

globberstack (glŏb′ŏr-stăk)

(n.) A stack of useless things.

Example: *"Hey Bill, what's this?" "Man, I don't know. Just throw it in that globberstack over there."*

gnilleps (gnĭl′lĕps)

(n.) An incorrectly spelled word; any malformation of words with letters in an unaccepted order.

Example: *Gnilleps is just plain fun to say.*

Origin: The reverse spelling of *spelling*.

Godvertising (gŏd'vər-tī'zĭng)

(n.) Any state-sanctioned public display intended to sell the idea of a supreme or omnipresent being.

Example: *Some people think the nativity scene in the town square is Godvertising.*

gondo (gŏn'dō)

(v.) To be gung-ho; to go crazy.

Example: *He was gondo during the war.*

Origin: Likely a variation on *gung-ho*, expressing enthusiasm, or possibly from *Gonzo*, one of the famous Muppet caricatures.

googlate (gü'gə'lāt)

(v.) To enter random words into a search engine out of sheer boredom or curiosity.

Example: *I spent the whole day at work googlating. It's kind of fun, and it looks like I'm really busy.*

GPX (gē-pē-ĕks)

(acro.) Global Positioning eX system; the habit of informing people where they've seen one's ex-lover. In this way one can track one's ex's movements without actually spotting them.

Example: *No, I don't think Richard is dating anyone new. My GPX system spotted him at the football game, the Pizza Plaza, and the mall, but he was only with Mike and Jack.*

Origin: Related to GPS (Global Positioning System).

gradue (gră'dü)

(n.) Anything gross and unidentifiable, usually sticky, that can be found almost everywhere.

Example: *Gradue can be found under the bed, on subway rails, stuck in one's teeth, or anywhere else one can think.*

Origin: A blending of *gross* and *residue.*

grandmalicious (grăn'mä-lĭsh'əs)

(adj.) Describing someone so cool that they become malicious and hateful.

Origin: From the medical term *grand mal seizure*, a serious convulsive seizure, and the word *malicious.*

gratisfaction (grăt'ĭs-făk'shən)

(n.) The state of being simultaneously gratified and satisfied.

Example: *I can't get no... gratisfaction.*

2. (n.) The satisfaction of getting something gratis.

graveorism (grāv'ə-rĭz'əm)

(n.) An aphorism that has passed away as truth and is now just a cliché.

Example: *"A penny saved is a penny earned." "Who cares? It's a penny! Quit lecturing me with your graveorisms."*

Origin: A play on the word *aphorism* and *grave* signifying its death or passing on, specifically referring to old sayings that no longer have relevance to modern life.

greencollar (grēn-kŏl'ər)
(adj.) Anyone who manages and works on a farm or agricultural concern.

grippage (grĭp'ĭj)
(n.) The measure of an object's grip.

gription (grĭp'shən)
(n.) Having the quality of grippage; an amount of grip.

Example: *Tires have gription instead of traction when they are getting a little bald.*

groaking (grōk'ĭng)
(v.) Literally, to consume or to drink. To consume a situation to the point that it becomes a part of one's self and one's self with it.

Origin: Like *grok*, to understand fully to a degree that most never achieve. To "grok in fullness" is to understand not just the situation at hand, but the actions and attitudes leading to it. This term was first put forth in the work of fiction "Stranger in a Strange Land" by Robert A. Heinlein.

2. (v.in.) To look at someone else's food, in the hope that she will offer a portion.

3. (n.) One who watches someone eat in hopes of being offered some of their scrumptious bounty.

grossling (grŏz'lĭng)
(n.) Any person or thing that is gross or does gross things.

grrok (gŭr-ōk)

(interj.) A reluctant acceptance of the situation at hand.

Example: *"Sorry, sir, we're all sold out." "Grrok."*

Origin: Combined form of *grr* and *okay*. Note the second *r*; not to be confused with *grok*.

gruntled (grŭn'tld)

(adj.) Contented; not postal; a person who is extremely satisfied with his working conditions.

Origin: Antonym of *disgruntled*.

guitarded (gĭ-tärd-ĕd)

(adj.) One who owns a guitar and displays it prominently to make himself appear more attractive, even though he has no idea how to play.

gumashification (gŭm-ăsh'ə-fĭ-kā'shən)

(n.) An act of putting a piece of used chewing gum in a dirty ashtray.

gurt (gûrt)

(v.) To cause pain while, at the same time, causing a feeling of pleasure; often related to the scratching of an itch.

Origin: The contraction of *good* and *hurt*.

gwallop (gwŏ-lŭp)

(v.) To swallow and gulp at the same time; to swallow a very large amount.

H

haargle (här'gəl)

(v.) The act of gargling with a hair in one's throat, resulting in a most unusual scream.

habitosis (hă-bĭ-tō'sĭs)

(n.) A disease affecting those who continually form habits out of every aspect of their life; the condition of making every action into a habit.

Origin: From the word *habit* and the Latin suffix *-osis*, a diseased or abnormal condition.

haggleable (hăg'əl-ə'bəl)

(adj.) Negotiable, especially as to price.

Example: *The sticker on this car is haggleable.*

hallucidate (hə-lü'sĭdāt')

(v.) To elucidate by means of a hallucination.

2. (v.) To have a hallucination that clears up something or illuminates the meaning of life, the universe and everything.

happifying (hăp'ə-fī'ĭng)

(adj.) Capable of making one happy.

Example: *To a woman, a gift of chocolate cake is happifying.*

Origin: A blending of *happy* and *gratifying*.

halficle (häf'ĭ-kəl)

(n.) A small cubicle or half of a large cubicle. Usually found in a call center.

happytitis (hăp'ē-tī'tĭs)

(n.) A disease usually brought on by the consumption of alcohol, usually lasting until one vomits.

headness (hĕd-nĕss)
(adj.) To have an abnormally large head.

Example: *His headness defied all bike helmet sizes.*

helloha (hĕ-lō'hä')
(interj.) An endearing greeting.

Origin: The blending of greetings between English, *hello*, and Hawaiian, *aloha*.

heredipet (hə-rĕd'ĭ-pĕt)
(n.) An unwanted pet inherited from a deceased relative or acquaintance, with a real or imagined obligation to care for the animal.

heredstupidity (hə'rĕd-stü-pĭd'ĭ-tē)
(n.) Inherited stupidity.

Example: *You're stupid because you received heredstupidity from your dad's side.*

hereticat (hĕr'ĭ-tĭ'căt)
(n.) A cat that chases dogs; or, a cat that likes to swim.

heteronormative (hĕt'ə-rō'nôr'mə-tĭv)
(adj.) An action which is deemed typical of heterosexuals.

Example: *Marriage is a heteronormative act.*

hiccaburp (hĭk'ə-bûrp)
(v.) To uncontrollably and simultaneously hiccup and burp. Sometimes called a *hicurp*.

hingent (hĭn'jənt)

(adj.) Determined or depending on another. Subject to another's jurisdiction.

Example: *Whether we go camping this weekend is hingent on whether Jake has a football game or not.*

hippocritamus (hĭp'ə-krĭt-ə'məs)

(n.) One who performs great acts of hypocrisy.

Origin: From *hypocrisy* and *hippopotamus*.

2. (n.) A big, fat hypocrite.

hipular (hĭp'yə-lər)

(adj.) Popular with the "hip" crowd.

Example: *iPods were hipular in 2004.*

hobnoblin (hŏb'nŏb'lĭn)

(n.) An obnoxious or mischievous, and overly familiar, acquaintance.

Example: *Dude, when are you going to shake Ron? He's a hobnoblin, and I'm not going if he comes along.*

Origin: From *hobnob*, associating familiarity, and *goblin*, a grotesque, mischievous folklore creature.

hobophobic (hō'bə-fō'bĭk)

(adj.) To be deathly afraid of hobos and/or homeless persons.

Example: *Mark doesn't like driving downtown, because he's hobophobic.*

hollymonger (hŏl'ē-mŭng'gər)

(n.) A person who forcibly insists that others participate in festivities and/or holiday activities.

Example: *I don't want to do "secret-Santa" this year, you hollymonger!*

Origin: From *holiday*, holy day or vacation, and *monger*, a peddler.

2. (v.) To emphatically insist that others have as much fun as one is (or should be) having.

Example: *I stopped by the office party because I needed to pick up my check and my boss wouldn't stop hollymongering me.*

honkin (hôngk-ĭn)

(adj.) Extremely large, very huge.

Example: *You see that big honkin tree over there? That's where I crashed my new car.*

Origin: A common phrase heard especially around New England and possibly other parts of the world likely referring to something that is loud and stands out, or that is so big that it's worth honking your horn over.

Note: Also *mahonkin*

horracious (hŏr'ə-shəs)

(adj.) Describing something so incredibly bad that one cannot even think of a word to describe it.

Origin: The blending of *horrible* and *atrocious*.

housewifier (hăüs'wĭ'fē-ûr)

(adj.) To become more of a housewife than previously; to act more on one's housewife instincts than others.

Example: *You should be glad your wife is housewifier than mine; I spend half my time cooking meals, doing laundry, and cleaning the bathrooms.*

2. (adj.) Having a strong impulse to clean, wash, or fold laundry, more so now than before.

hoxy (hŏk'sē)

(adj.) Something that is both hot and sexy.

Example: *I was going to break up with Kathy last night, but she was wearing those hoxy leather boots.*

hu (hyü')

(pron.) A 3rd person gender-neutral pronoun. Its brevity and morphological structure (one open syllable: a consonant + a vowel) make it similar to other 3rd person pronouns — a typical, easily recognizable member of this class: he, she, hu.

Example: *An employee may choose to cover only huself and hus child or any number of children.*

Origin: A clipping from "human" (like "flu" from "influenza"). The derivative forms of "hu": reflexive "huself," possessive "hus," and objective "hu."

humilify (hyü-mĭl'ĭ-fī')

(v.) Gently humiliating; putting someone in her place by citing an example of her incompetence.

humography (hyü'mŏg'rə-fē)

(n.) A funny story that is only funny to those who were there. If told anywhere else, or at a different time, it becomes dull.

Example: *Joe, that story was funny when were in the bar and finishing the third pitcher. This morning it's just a humography.*

Origin: From *humor* and *geography*.

humongify (hyü-mŏng'gə-fī')

(v.) To make extremely large or enormous.

Example: *On the big screen, that girl's posterior was humongified by a factor of ten!*

humstinker (hŭm-stĭnk'ər)

(n.) One who is extraordinary smelly, and who has probably not used deodorant in a considerably long time.

Example: *You are NOT getting into the car until you take off your football equipment and take a shower, you humstinker!*

hydroholic (hī'drə-hô'lĭk)

(n.) A person who is addicted to water. This person must drink at least two litres (approx. eight cups) of water a day, and, in order to match her mood, choose bottled water based on flavor and mineral content.

Origin: From *hydro-*, of water, and from *-holic*, signifying addiction to.

hypnoxia (hĭp-nŏk'sē-ə)

(n.) A condition described as having extremely irritating qualities.

Example: *Man, she's hypnoxious! I don't know anyone with a worse case of hypnoxia.*

Origin: A play on the medical term *hypnoxia*, low blood oxygen level; and the word *obnoxious*.

I

iconoblast (ī'kŏn'ō'blăst)

(v.) To punctuate one's instant message with an excess of icons.

ID1OT (ī-dē-těn-tē)

(adj.) Describes a computer "error," which is really user incompetence. Commonly used in computer circles.

Example: *Yeah, Ms. Wormwood made an ID10T mistake.*

Origin: ID10T looks like idiot. The added 10 implies a binary or digital origin.

ideality (ī'dē-ăl'ĭ-tē)

(n.) Frequently the opposite of reality. A dimension only spoken of in textbooks and lectures. While greatly desired, an ideality never seems to become reality.

Origin: Not to be confused with other definitions of ideality, this term actually is derived from *ideal* and *reality*, the real dimension or existence in which we live.

idiology (ĭd'ē-ŏl'ə-jē)

(n.) Political dogma espoused by anyone whose intellectual credentials are derived solely from his experience in professional sports or the entertainment industry.

Origin: The contraction of *idiot* and *ideology*.

ifnik (ĭf-nĭk)

(n.) Any person whose life, habits, and thinking are constructed conditionally.

Example: *Don't ask him what he's going to do. As a typical ifnik, he will give you a dozen "ifs."*

igmo (ĭg'mō)

(n.) An ignorant person; abbreviated form of ignoramus.

2. IGMO. (acro.) I've Got My Orders. A rueful to matter-of-fact commentary by a person executing a decision of others that may not seem sensible to the speaker or addressee.

Origin: Military slang.

ignorement (ĭg-nôr-mənt)

(n.) The act or process of ignoring.

Example: *I hoped to receive forgiveness but instead was met with suspicion and ignorement.*

Origin: A noun that signifies ignoring something or somebody, corresponding to the verb *ignore*, but different from *ignorance*.

ignorimagrant (ĭg'nər-ĭm'ĭ-grənt)

(adj.) An out-of-towner who doesn't know how to drive according to the local laws; a really bad driver.

imaccentate (ĭm-ăk'sĕn-tāt')

(v.) The act of subconsciously imitating the accent of the person to whom one is speaking, thereby causing the person to first become puzzled, and then slightly offended when they come to believe they are being made fun of.

Origin: From *imitate* and *accent*.

IMbiguity (ī-ĕm-bĭ-gyü'ĭ-tē)

(n.) Ambiguity caused by the nature of instant messaging and its lack of tone, context, or other visual expressions.

Example: *I really thought Jane was mad at me, but it was just the IMbiguity of her messages.*

imbourbonated (ĭm-bûr'bə-nāt'ĕd)

(adj.) To be drunk on the mash.

Origin: The blending of *intoxicated* and *bourbon*.

imporntant (ĭm-pôrn'tnt)

(adj.) Describing the type of documents that should be backed up prior to having work done on one's computer.

Example: *I had to get all those imporntant astrology documents off my computer first.*

Origin: From *important* and from the more recent use of the word *porn*, any article or item of importance to a particular interest group.

indisuggestion (ĭn'dĭ-səg-jĕs'chən)

(n.) Any entirely useless remedy for getting rid of gas, or indigestion; possibly through hypnosis.

inebrionics (ĭn-ē'brē-ŏn'ĭks)

(n.) A nonstandard form of American English spoken by individuals under the extreme influence of mind altering chemicals, usually indigenous to certain stretches of sidewalks and public establishments.

Origin: A blending of *Inebriated* and *phonics*.

ineptiphobia (ĭn-ĕp'tĭ-fō'bē-ə)

(n.) An abnormal fear of being inept.

infinition (ĭn'fə-nĭ-shən)

(n.) An infinite process of defining something that cannot be fully or precisely defined; an endless list of possible definitions.

Example: *Certain fluid concepts in their emergent state are subject to infinition—infinite dispersal of their meaning— rather than to definition. To infine is to suggest the infinity of possible definitions of a certain term or concept and therefore to problematize its meaning and the possibility or the benefit of defining it. If definition circumscribes a specific conceptual area, then infinition releases the concept from restricting demarcations and places it in an indeterminate zone.*

Origin: From *definition* and *infinity*.

infomoron (ĭn'fō-môr'ŏn')

(n.) An infomercial stand-in specialized in the task of showing the audience just how difficult commonplace tools or equipment can be to use, giving them ample reason to buy the newer, supposedly superior product being advertised. A certified professional will often demonstrate low manual dexterity, confusion with simple tasks, and a disastrous storage system that leaves him unable to locate the things he needs.

Example: *Let's watch the infomoron unsuccessfully staple papers together.*

Origin: From *infomercial*, an informational commercial about a new product, and *moron*.

infotainjugal (ĭn'fə-tān'jə-gəl)

(adj.) Describing salacious material presented on mass media as informational and consumed as entertainment by its audience.

Example: *That PBS documentary on hormones in teenagers was really infotainjugal, wouldn't you say?*

Origin: The combination of *informational, entertainment,* and *conjugal*.

inscape (ĭn-skāp')

(v.) To escape into one's self; to escape inwardly.

Example: *I'm going to inscape from this classroom and into my mind. At least that way I won't get in trouble.*

insparation (ĭn-spä-rā'shən)

(n.) Thinking up a great idea while sitting in a spa or sauna.

inspectigate (ĭn-spĕkt'ĭ-gāt')

(v.) To investigate closely with the intensity of an inspection.

Example: *I was really nervous while that customs guy inspectigated my trumpet case, where I had stuck the bootleg tapes I was trying to sneak into the country.*

insufferior (ĭn-sə-fîr'ē-ər)

(adj.) To feel inferior or insufficient.

Example: *When James talks about his old girlfriends, I feel really insufferior.*

integritous (ĭn-tĕg'rĭ-təs)

(adj.) Characterized by integrity.

internet leech (ĭn'tər-nĕt' lēch)

(n.) A person who uses only free AOL trial disks to access the internet, without ever paying for it.

interrobang (!?) (ĭn-tĕr'ə-băng)

(n.) A combination of a question mark and an exclamation point or the appearance of both right next to each other.

Example: *What do you think you're doing!?*

Origin: From *interrogate*, to question, and *bang*, a short name for an exclamation point.

intertwingle (ĭn'tər-twĭng'gəl)

(v.) To mingle and intertwine with others.

Example: *I hope to intertwingle and meet new people at the party.*

Intpossibility (ĭnt'pŏs'ə–bĭl'ĭ–tĕ)

(n.) Something that is a possible to do over the Internet.

Example: *We knew we'd never get tickets over the phone, but getting them online was definitely an intpossibility.*

iono (ī-ō-nō)

(contr.) Shortened form of "I don't know."

Example: *Iono if I want to go to breakfast.*

iridiscance (ĭr'ĭ-dĭs'kəns)

(n.) The property of CDs and DVDs that causes them to emit a spectrum pattern whenever a light is shined on them.

irkutated (ûr'kĭ-tā'tĕd)

(adj.) Past the point of being both irked and irritated.

irritainment (ĭr'ĭ-tān'mənt)

(n.) Entertainment that makes one irritated.

Example: *I hate irritainment like the O.J. trial and all those reality shows.*

J

JABUPS (jä-bŭps)

(acro.) Jargon Articulated By Unintelligible Public Servants.

Example: *No, I didn't rent a new P.O. box — I couldn't translate the clerk's JABUPS.*

jampage (jămˈpājʹ)

(v.) The screaming and dancing rampage one goes on when one jams or stubs a body part on a household object.

Example: *Mom went into a major jampage when she smacked her toe on the open oven door.*

2. (n.) A jamming session that is rampageous enough to make the listener believe that the musician is crazy.

Japlish (jăpˈlĭsh)

(n.) The mistranslation of Japanese words or phrases into English.

2. (adj.) Of or relating to a language in which both English and Japanese words are used together in order to express a meaning.

jeatjet (jētˈjĕt)

(contr.) Have you eaten yet?

Example: *Hey, we're going for the two-for-one special down at Burger Barn. Jeatjet?*

Jesufied (gē-zə-fīd)

(v.in.) To be martyred. To take the rap for something knowing you will get in the least amount of trouble.

Example: *Knowing his friends would get in more trouble than he, Ray Jesufied himself and told the police officer all the booze was his.*

jimbly (jĭm'blē)

(adv.) Describing nostalgic, childish, or immature fun.

Example: *All of our parents jimbly played a game of sardines together.*

jobsworth jŏbs'wûrth')

(n.) A measure of a task in comparison to a job's worth. Usually refers to a task that, in order to complete, requires compensation above and beyond a single job's worth.

Example: *I can't write the boss' speech by tomorrow morning; it's more than a jobsworth.*

jogma (jôg'mə)

(n.) The tenets, secrets, and mysteries surrounding jogging.

Example: *Jogma states that running shoes should be replaced about every six months.*

jokative (jō'kə-tĭv)

(adj.) Describes one who expresses himself frequently through jokes.

Examples: *John was unusually jokative today.*
Don't get mad, I was just being jokative!

judder (jŭd'ər)

(v.in.) A cross between a jerk and a shudder.

Example: *I told the mechanic, "When I roll up my car window, it judders."*

jumpskiffling (jŭmp-skĭf'əl-ĭng)

(v.in.) To jump around like a complete moron because of something stupid.

Example: *Because her chicken laid an egg, Rosie started jumpskiffling!*

Origin: A cross between *jumping*, *skipping*, and *shuffling*.

junkword (jŭngk-wûrd)

(n.) Any word or unword submitted to a slang or unword dictionary that is either already a real word or is not worthy of being called an unword.

Examples: *Some junkwords are: Cute (a real word), Vanessishot (meaning "Vanessa is hot," appears to be created out of drunkenness and is not very useful in many situations. How many Vanessas do you know?)*

Origin: Often junkwords exist because someone doesn't understand the concept of unwords or there is no good logical explanation to their submission.

justifiction (jŭs'tə-fĭk'shən)

(n.) The use of false or fraudulent reasoning to excuse, explain, or defend an act.

Example: *President Bush's justifiction for the Iraq War was the presence of WMDs. His justifiction for keeping it going is that he wants to give democracy to Iraqis. What's he going to think of next?*

Origin: The blending of *justification* and *fiction*.

K

kabomb (kŭ-bŏm)

(n.) Anything that makes a satisfying kaboom sound.

Example: *Johnny made a great kabomb from a big roll of bubble wrap.*

Ken Jennings (kĕn jĕn'ĭngs)

(n.) A genius; someone who is smarter than all of his cohorts.

Example: *That Ken Jennings keeps answering all the teacher's questions. What a brown noser!*

Origin: From Jeopardy celebrity Ken Jennings. As a famous record-holder for the longest winning streak (74 wins) on the game show, *Ken Jennings* has become synonymous with *genius*.

2. (adj.) Describing anything that is smart or that demonstrates one's genius.

Example: *Wow, that idea is Ken Jennings.*

kewl (kül, kyül)

(adj.) Slang. Totally awesome; great or exciting.

Origin: An alternate spelling of the 1970s term *cool*. There are suggestions that this spelling originated from the popular "1337" (leet, elite) speech used among today's online pop culture. The replacement of *oo* with *ew* suggests that the person using the term is cooler than someone who uses the normal spelling.

keybergoo (kē'bər-gō)

(n.) The sticky gunk on the keyboard of a computer or musical instrument after food, drink, or some other sticky substance is dropped on it.

Example: *Dude, you squirted ketchup on my new keyboard! Now I'll be dealing with keybergoo for weeks!*

kharmageddon (kär'mə-gĕd'n)

(n.) When one is paid immediately for all the bad things one has done in one's life.

Origin: From *armageddon*, a catastrophic conflict, and *karma*.

kipple (kĭp'əl)

(n.pl.) Any collection of useless objects. Over time, kipple will reproduce itself if not attended to.

Example: *We found a lot of kipple in the attic of that old pack rat's home.*

Origin: This term comes from chapter six of the novel "Blade Runner" written by Phillip K. Dick in 1968.

kneebow (nē-bō)

(n.) The elbow of one's leg.

See also: Kneepit

kneekle (nē'kəl)

(n.) The portion of one's leg extending from the knee to the ankle. It is referred to in this manner if the person displays excess fat that essentially hides the calf area.

kneepit (nē'pĭt')

(n.) Area of space behind the knee.

Origin: A variation on *armpit* to refer to the similarly shaped area behind one's knee.

See also: Kneebow

kookookachoo (kü-kü-kă-chü)

(interj.) A phrase used to express happiness. Sometimes yelled after a random act simply when one desires to be obnoxious.

Origin: From the popular 1967 Beatles song, "I Am the Walrus."

koolio (cü'lē-ō)

(adj.) Cool; expressing happiness or joy.

Example: "I'm done with all my exams!" "Koolio, dude, let's go to the bar."

Origin: From the phrase, *cool*, coined in the mid-60s to early-70s that has slowly become outdated. This newer form provides a rather hip and trendy, yet timeless expression of the familiar phrase. Possible Spanish roots are implied by the *-io*.

See also: Kewl

L

lamien (lām-ē'ən)

(n.) A person purported to be evil and frightening, but who is simply lame.

Example: *Freddy may have been scary at one time, but now he's just a lamien.*

Origin: From *lame* and *Damien*, antagonist from "The Omen" films whose name resembles demon.

lapdog (lăp-dôg)

(n.) A submissive individual who is socially dependent on the leader of the group. The lapdog will always do what the group leader asks without question.

Example: *Edward is Dee's lapdog; he doesn't do anything without her permission.*

later tots (lā'tər tŏts)

(n.) Tater tots that were left in a refrigerator for over a week and have started to turn weird colors.

latersohinip (lā'shĭr-səh'ən-ĭp)

(n.) A mixed-up relationship.

Origin: A scrambled spelling of the term *relationship*.

leet (lēt)

(adj.) Elite; used in the computing world.

Example: *That new source code is leet!*

Origin: Derived from *elite*.

leetspeak (lēt-spēk)

(n.) A form of written, and sometimes verbal, language used in the realm of savvy computer users, hackers, and kiddies. In written language, words are often spelled with a portion of numeric symbols used to represent similar looking letter counterparts.

Example: *1337, l337 and l33t are three common ways the term* leet *is spelled in leetspeak.*

Origin: From *leet*, *elite*, and *speak*.

lesbertising (lĕz'bər-tī'zĭng)

(n.) A notice or announcement in a public medium, meant to appeal to lascivious males, which uses two or more young women in a sexually suggestive pose to promote a product, service, or event.

lesbionic (lĕz'bē-ŏn'ĭk)

(adj.) Anything having female homosexual traits and/or lesbian qualities.

Example: *That's a very lesbionic hair style.*

2. (adj.) Something done specifically by or for lesbians.

lessless (lĕs'lĭs)

(adj.) Without; not having even a lesser amount.

libits (lĭ'bĭts)

(n.pl.) Any piece of bread from the front or back of a loaf that no one wishes to eat.

Origin: From *loaf* and *niblet*, a small piece of.

lickaspatch (lĭk-ə'spăch')

(v.) The act of licking the spatula after baking.

Example: *Many are familiar with well-known lickaspatchian techniques.*

linkrot (lĭngk-rŏt)

(v.) When a link on a webpage becomes extinct.

Example: *His website linkrotted shortly after he started redesigning it.*

linner (lĭn'ər)

(n.) A meal eaten early in the evening as a combination of lunch and dinner.

Origin: Much like *brunch*, the combination of breakfast and lunch.

liquordized (lĭk'ər-dĭz'd)

(v.tr.) To be drunk on alcohol.

loanation (lō-nā'shən)

(n.) Money loaned, typically to a close relative, without the expectation of being repaid.

loft queen (lôft kwēn)

(n.) A regal, mature woman of the city.

Origin: From the stately or lofty reputation that a successful city woman displays.

lonolik (lŭ-nō'lĭk)

(v.) To truly love someone as a friend and yet not actually like the person in a romantic way.

Example: *"Wow! Alex, I love her to death, but I don't like her like her." "So do you lonolik her?"*

loseronic (lü'zə'rŏn'ĭk)

(adj.) Describing a complete and utter loser.

Origin: The blending of *loser* and *moronic*.

losery (lü'zər'ē)

(adj.) Having the characteristics of a loser.

Origin: The addition of suffix -y to transform *loser* into a measure of one's quality.

2. (adj.) Decidedly not a winner.

3. (adj.) Deserving of merciless ridicule.

lostivity (lôstĭv'ĭ-tē)

(n.) State of being lost.

lovedicing (lŭv-dīc'ĭng)

(v.) Gambling on the assumption that one can lead another person on for an extended period of time without developing deepening feelings for said person.

Example: *Jack has been lovedicing his relationship with Jill as they both have gone to fetch water each day.*

Origin: From *love* and *dicing*, gambling.

2. (v.) Gambling on the, possibly wrongful, assumption that one can be in love with two people at the same time.

lovedom (lŭv'dəm)

(n.) The realm of love, the totality of loving emotions and attitudes.

Example: *The King of England, Edward VIII, was that rare romantic who challenged society by trading his kingdom for lovedom.*

lowjack (lō'jăk')

(v.) To steal someone's slow means of transportation.

Example: *Hundreds of rollerblades, scooters, skateboards, and pogo sticks were lowjacked this weekend in a high-profile heist.*

Origin: The inverse of *highjack*, which commonly refers to the theft of a car, airplane, or other fast transportation.

ludicrism (lü'dĭ-krĭz'əm)

(n.) A distinctive doctrine, system, or theory that is laughable or hilarious because of its obvious absurdity.

Example: *The Flying Spaghetti Monster is true ludicrism.*

lumb duck (lŭm dŭk)

(n.) An extreme form of dumb luck.

lupper (lŭp'ər)

(n.) A meal taken between lunch and supper.

2. (n.) A hybrid of a mid-day meal and an evening repast.

See also: *linner*

M

madamismness (măd'ə-mĭz'əm'nĕss)

(adj.) Describing someone who is supercilious, overbearing, and/or haughtily proud. Often descriptive of certain types of women who are not divas.

Example: *There was a certain madamismness about her.*

mahonkin (mə'hôngk-ĭn)

(adj.) Humongous; extremely huge; so big that there is none larger.

Example: *You have one mahonkin sub in your car!*

Origin: From *massive* and *honkin*.

See also: *honkin*

malbingophobia (môl-bĭng'gō'fō'bē-ə)

(n.) The fear among some bingo players that they have incorrectly marked a square, and calling "bingo" could cause them not victory, but public humiliation.

Origin: From Latin *malus*, badly, *bingo*, and Greek *phobos*, fear.

malmonodemsome (măl-mŏn'ō-dĕm'səm)

(adj.) Full of bad, single people.

Example: *This is a very malmonodemsome cruise ship.*

Origin: From Latin *malus*, badly, from Greek *monos*, single or one, *dem-* from *demographic*, and from Old English *sum*, akin to.

mandals (măn'dls)

(n.pl.) Open-toe sandals worn by men.

manimal (măn'ə-məl)

(n.) A person who resembles an animal, usually a monkey or gorilla.

Example: *Check out that guy's hairy back. What a manimal!*

manorexic (măn'ə-rĕk'sĭk)

(adj.) Characterizing a male who eats an extremely large amount of food and yet gains no weight.

Example: *Renan ate that whole pie and he is still manorexic.*

manscape (măn'skāp')

(n.) A term of admiration towards members of the male gender, especially in reference to a group of males.

Example: *I love to watch the volleyball players at the beach on weekends, and just sit and admire the manscape.*

2. (v.) When a man grooms his body hair.

Example: *He just got his eyebrows waxed for the first time and is now considering waxing his chest. Manicures are one thing, but I am afraid his manscaping is getting out of control.*

manssiere (măn-zîr')

(n.) A bra for a guy.

margraine (mär'grān')

(n.) The blinding pain one suffers from drinking margarita slush too quickly.

Masshole (măs-hōl')

(n.) The nut who goes 90 mph all the time, cuts others off any chance he gets, and travels a foot behind another's bumper even when he has the opportunity to pass.

Origin: From the unsettling methods of driving experienced while in range of a Massachusetts driver.

mattricide (măt'rĭ-sĭd')
  (n.) The act of removing the "do not remove" tag on a
  mattress, thus somehow rendering the mattress invalid.

mayonize (mā'ə-nīz)
  (v.) To apply mayonnaise to an item to be used in the
  making of a sandwich or other such food.

McFinch (mĭk-fĭnch)
  (n.) A small bird whose natural habitat is in the parking lot
  of a fast food restaurant, and does not seem to exist in any
  other part of the world.

McSkimming (mĭk-skĭm'ĭng)

(v.) Pocketing cash orders at the drive-up window.

meandrathal (mē-ăn'dər-thôl')

(n.) Any person in an exhausted state of mind who wanders aimlessly, sometimes with low blood-sugar, in a shopping mall, video store, or the like.

Origin: A derivation of *neanderthal*, an extinct Homo sapiens species or subspecies, and *meander*, to wander.

mediacracy (mē'dē-ə-krə-sē)

(n.) Government, usually indirectly, by the popular media; often a result of democracy going awry. A system in which politicians stop thinking and begin listening exclusively to the media regarding what the important issues are and what they should do about them.

Origin: A play on *democracy* and *news media*; possible reference to being *mediocre*.

meetnik (mēt-nĭk)

(n.) A person who enjoys meetings and other administrative events and attends as many of them as possible.

Example: *Being socially active is one thing, meeting for the sake of meeting is another. I try to stay away from meetniks for whom getting together is an end in itself. Meeting without meaning is worse than meaning without meeting.*

Origin: From *meet* and *-nik,* a suffix to describe anyone who has a large level of conformity, such as in *peacenik* or *beatnik*.

megapixures (mĕg'ə-pĭks'ərs)

(n.pl.) Pictures taken with a digital camera or prints made from digital files.

Origin: From digital buzz-term *megapixels* and *pictures*.

melty (məl-tē)

(adj.) Of a melted consistancy; being partially melted.

Example: *The s'more was deliciously melty.*

Origin: Recently used in televised Taco Bell ads for their "Cheesy Gordita Crunch."

menuspect (mĕn'yü-spĕkt)

(v.) To look at what other people have ordered in a restaurant while being taken to one's seat by the hostess.

menwheel (mĕn'hwēl)

(n.) The occasional urge to use one's mouse wheel to make a menu slide up from the bottom or side of the screen. This behavior always results in the accidental scrolling of a document because menus do not work that way in today's computing world.

Example: *After hours of work, Jim tried to check the time on his task menu, but instead found himself in menwheel as his 500-page thesis flew by him.*

metabusy (mĕt'ə-bĭz'ē)

(adj.) Being extremely busy, usually because of an inability to complete a primary task.

Example: *Since my hard drive crashed, I am metabusy trying to finish my reports.*

minging (mĭng'ĭn)

(v.tr.) British slang. Foul and utterly disgusting. Something physically repellant visually, nasally, or otherwise. Usually used as reference to an object or act.

Example: *Long-expired food unearthed from the fridge that is now nearing almost radioactive levels of instability/mutation: "This is completely minging cheese."*

Origin: Possible derivation from *mange*, a parasitic skin disease of mammals.

misanthropism (mĭs-ăn'thrə-pĭz'əm)

(n.) The belief that humanity in general is rubbish; that humanity has a grim future; that people in general are evil and that one should stay away from them.

Origin: A reversal of the term *theanthropism*, a belief that attributes humanity toward God, and based on the word *misanthropist*, to hate or mistrust humanity.

miserability (mĭz'ər-ə-bĭl'ĭ-tē)

(n.) The measurement of how miserable one is at any given moment; the maximum level of one's ability to be miserable.

Example: *Would you say your miserability was relatively high after your house fell into a sinkhole?*

misunderestimate (mĭs'ŭn'dər-ĕs'tə-māt')

(v.) To misunderstand someone's behavior, writing, or speech in such a way as to underestimate that person.

Origin: Made popular by George W. Bush during his first campaign for presidency.

monoemotionistic (mŏnō-ĭ-mō'shən-ĭs'tĭk)
(adj.) Capable of feeling or having only a single emotion at a time.

monopulate (mə-nŏp'yə-lāt')
(v.tr.) To manipulate others into accepting a certain viewpoint or idea by controlling a conversation.

morical (môr'ĭ-kəl)
(adj.) Possessing a strong moral value.

Example: *This movie is more morical than the last one we watched.*

moronasaurus (môr'ŏn'ə-sôr'əs)
(n.) Someone whose stupidity has, or should have, caused them to become extinct.

motate (mō'tāt)
(v.) To leave.

Example: *Let's motate.*

mousecurse (măüs-kûrs)
(n.) A curse afflicting a user whose mouse pointer overshoots its intended target as many as a dozen times in a row.

mousecurser (măüs-kûrs'ər)
(n.) Someone who shouts at a mouse for overshooting the intended target.

muckle (mŭk'l)

(v.) To smother with something sticky or dirty. To muckle something up, as to mess it up completely.

Origin: From *muck* and *meddle*. Possibly related to *muggle*.

muggle (mŭg'gəl)

(v.) To smother or cover completely. Used mainly when one is muggling another, or completely smothering someone with signs of affection, but to that person's annoyance.

Origin: Possibly from *mug*, to assault.

mulligal (mŭl'ĭ-gəl)

(n.) In golf, a provisional mulligan. A mulligan is a second shot, without penalty, when the golfer is unhappy with the first. If, however, the mulligan is worse than the first shot, it becomes a mulligal and the player uses his first ball.

Origin: A crossing of *mulligan* and *optional*.

mumism (mŭm-ĭz'əm)

(n.) Any useless information a mother gives her child; formally called "old wives' tales."

Example: *"So what mumism have you learned today?" "If you eat carrots you will be able to see in the dark."*

murfed (mûrfĕd)

(v.tr.) To be victimized by Mr. Murphy of Murphy's Law.

Example: *While the weatherman predicted sun, we got murfed by floods.*

Origin: From *Murphy's Law*: what can go wrong will go wrong.

murphyglobule (mûr'fē-glŏb'yül)

(n.) The inevitable glob of food that drips onto a clean white surface, often one's shirt.

Example: *Everything was going fine on our date until I took my last bite of chowder and got murphyglobules all over.*

Origin: The union of *Murphy's Law* and *globule*.

murse (mûrs)

(n.) A male nurse.

muxup (mŭks'ŭp')

(v.) To mix and muck things up at the same time.

Example: *Why did you have to go and muxup things again?*

N

nanobus (năn'ə-bəs)

(adj.) Extremely small; dwarfish.

Origin: A more dainty form of *nanous*, dwarfish.

narf (närf)

(interj.) An exclamation emitted when one's brain farts and sound deploys.

Origin: An infamous expression used by the unintelligent sidekick of "The Brain," Pinky, as seen in the popular cartoon "Pinky and the Brain," produced by Steven Spielberg.

nast (năst)

(n.) Filth; usually, but not necessarily, identifiable.

Example: *After the party there was nast all over my carpet.*

2. (interj.) Used to express disgust or offense.

Example: *Aww, nast!*

nastola (năs'tŏ'lă)

(adj.) Describing something that is nasty.

NCMO (nĭk-mō, ĕn-sē-ĕm-ō)

(acr.) Non-Committal Make Out. The act of two people getting together with an unwritten or other agreement that they will make out but not develop a relationship.

Example: *"Hey baby, want a little NCMO?" says Richard.*

nervert (nûr'vûrt)

(adj.) A computer nerd whose skills are dedicated to surfing for pornographic materials.

Example: *Josh: "Wow, check out this Chinese porn site." Jim: "Josh, you're such a nervert!"*

netoriety (nĕ'tə-rī'ĭ-tē)

(n.) A measure of one's reputation throughout the Internet.

Example: *Dude, don't order the software from that guy. He's netorious for selling faulty code.*

Origin: The combination of *net*, referring to the Internet, and *notoriety*.

nevways (nĕv-wāz')

(adv.) Sometimes; often spoken in a cute, sarcastic voice.

Example: *Joe: "Do you like watching me play video games, honey?" Jen: "Nevways, my honey-bunny."*

Origin: A crossing of *never* and *not always*.

newify (nü'ə-fī')

(v.) To make something that was old new again by refurbishing, painting, repairing, or some other activity.

Example: *David is going to newify that old table he found in the alley by painting it, then he's going to newify his car by fixing the rust holes.*

nifterrificalabulous (nĭf'tə-rĭf'ĭ-kəl-ăb'yə-ləs)

(adj.) Being nifty, terrific, radical, and fabulous; injected into conversation to express one's extreme like for something.

Example: *That ice cream with toasted coconut, whipped cream, hot fudge, and a cherry on top tasted nifterrificalabulous.*

ninjury (nĭn'jə-rē)

(n.) An injury, usually a pulled groin muscle, sustained while trying to show off a cool martial arts move.

Example: *Only a martial arts dweeb like you could sustain three ninjuries in one year!*

Origin: A blending of *ninja* and *injury*.

noggin'noddin (nŏg'ĭn nŏd'ĭn)

(v.) A periodic bobbing of one's head when one is about to doze off, often recurring in regular succession either in a rhythmical or intermittent pattern; a sign that one is too inactive or tired to stay awake.

Example: *While driving at night, Jeff started noggin'noddin*

nonversation (nŏn'vər-sā'shən)

(n.) A conversation between two or more people of absolutely no value, such as a discussion of the weather.

noob (nüb)

(n.) Someone who is a beginner to a particular activity; most commonly used for people new to online games and unaware of gamers' nettiquette.

Example: *Ninja: "Someone's begging for a free weapon."*
Wizard: "Don't mind him, he's just a noob."

Origin: A more *leet* form of *newbie*, or someone who is new.

noon-thirty (nün-thûr'tē)

(n.) Twelve-thirty.

noonsense (nün'sĕns')

(n.) The keen ability to know what time of day it is based on a feeling.

nostralgia (nŏs'trăl'gə)

(n.) A reminder of one's past brought on by a familiar smell.

Example: *Wow, I got major nostralgia when I walked by the school and got a big whiff of cafeteria food.*

not-a-date (nŏt-ə-dāt)

(adj.) An activity that closely resembles a date in every way except that it is not actually a date. A not-a-date activity can either be a purely platonic occurrence or can occur with a not-boyfriend or not-girlfriend.

Example: *Kevin and Francine went to enjoy a not-a-date night at the movies.*

not-boyfriend (nŏt-boi'frĕnd')

(n.) A person who behaves in every way like one's boyfriend, but is not romantically involved. These people will gladly take an offer for a not-a-date activity.

Note: *Not-girlfriend also common.*

0

obeseist (ō-bēs'ĭst)

(n.) One who is discriminatory or acts disrespectfully towards obese people.

obliviot (ə-blĭv'ĭ-ət)

(n.) Someone who is completely unaware of his or her idiocy.

oblivity (ə-blĭv'ĭ-tē)

(v.) The measure of one's complete lack of attention to one's surroundings.

Example: *Due to his oblivity at the baseball game, Joe was struck in the head by a foul ball.*

obnoxion (ŏb-nŏk-shən)

(n.) Someone or something that is considered obnoxious.

2. (n.) Any obnoxious material; an atom of obnoxious behavior.

obstetricize (ŏb-stĕt'rĭ-sīz')

(v.) To shun a baby.

Origin: From *ostracize* and *obstetrics*, a branch of medicine dealing with pregnancy and childbirth.

obvium (ŏb'vē-əm)

(n.) Something that is obvious.

offshource (ôf'shôrs')

(v.) To send jobs to another country.

Origin: Portmanteau of *offshore* and *outsource*.

oinkmeal (oingk'mēl')

(n.) Instant oatmeal.

Origin: From *oink*, in this context denoting something that can be quickly prepared and eaten, and *oatmeal*.

oldfolkals (ōld-fōl'kăls)

(n.pl.) The eyeglasses one needs when one can no longer see anything more than 10 feet away, or one's arms appear to have shrunk too much to hold the newspaper at a reasonable reading distance.

Origin: From *bifocals*, eyeglasses, and from *old folks*, members of an older generation of people.

omniloathe (ŏm-nĭl'ōth, ŏm'nĭ-lōth)

(n.) An all-encompassing feeling of disgust or repugnance toward a subject.

omnivolent (ŏm'nĭ-və-lənt)

(adj.) Uncertain about absolutely everything; hesitant to move in any direction at all.

oneirogenic (ō-nī'rō-jĕn'ĭk)

(adj.) Having a propensity to appear in somebody's dreams.

Example: *Some people are photogenic while others are oneirogenic. A person who is plain and unnoticeable in real life may haunt our dreams and imagination.*

Origin: Greek *oneiros* dream, and *genic* forming.

onosecond (ō-nō-sĕk'ənd)

(n.) The period of time one spends between pressing the send button and then realizing that he really shouldn't have sent that e-mail message.

Origin: From the interjection *Oh no!*

onycheldigger (ŏn-ĭk'əl-dĭg'ər)

(n.) Any object used as a tool to clean the disgusting build-up of grime under the fingernails. Usually something found nearby, like a push pin or a sharp corner of a folded peice of paper.

Origin: *Onych* comes from the Greek word *onyx*, which means claw or fingernail.

optoblur cycle (ŏp'tō-blûr sī'kəl)

(n.) An occasional seven- to eight-second vision loss, where one's eyes blur out of focus and then back, losing all aspects of color and detail; often occurring in the morning, as one's eyes adjust to the light.

orbituary (ôr'bĭch'ōō–ĕr'ē)

(n.) Worldwide coverage of a person's death.

outgeek (ăüt-gēk)

(v.tr.) The action of a geek being outdone or exposed to an event, occurrence, or activity that is even geekier or dorkier than he or she is.

Example: *Sure, he collects action figures, reads comic books, and goes to Trekkie conventions, but even he gets outgeeked when it comes to "Transformers."*

outsourcery (ăüt-sôr'sə-rē)

(n.) The all-too-frequently tragic belief that all business problems can magically be solved by outsourcing.

Origin: From *outsource*, to send work to an outside group to cut costs, and from *sorcery*, magic or witchcraft.

P

padawan (pă'də-wän)

(n.) An apprentice who undergoes intensive training under an experienced mentor.

Origin: From the popular Star Wars saga.

paddywaggle (păd'ē-wăg-əl)

(v.) To screw around or cause trouble.

Example: *Hey, Patrick, if you paddywaggle on your way home, you'll get run over!*

Origin: From *paddy wagon*, a van used to transport prisoners. Paddy, short for Patrick, was used as a derogatory term for someone of Irish descent.

pairification (pâr'ə-fĭ-kā'shən)

(n.) The coupling of two objects, ideas, or elements in a particular course of study.

Example: *The pairification of solids and voids in the stone wall creates wonderful moments of light.*

2. (n.) The coupling or adjoining of multiple (most often two) closely related ideas, elements or objects in a particular course of study.

3. (n.) The putting together of two similar objects.

palpicake (pāl-pĭ'kāk)

(n.) To test baked goods for freshness by prodding.

pantyho (păn'tē-hō)

(n.) One leg of a pair of pantyhose.

papertexting (pā'pər-tĕkst'ĭng)

(v.) To jot down a note on a scrap of paper, take a camera phone snapshot of it, and picture message (MMS) it over to a friend; often more expressive and expensive than regular SMS text.

parannoy (păr'ə-noi')

(v.) The act of annoying someone in such a fashion that makes him or her paranoid.

parcehole (pärs'hōl)

(n.) An irritating person who works in the post office or shipping service.

parkma (pärk-mə)

(n.) The uncanny luck of someone to be able to find a good parking spot everywhere she goes.

Example: *Let Jenny drive. She has great parkma, so we'll find a spot right in front of the theater.*

Origin: From *park* and *karma*, the Hindu measurement of one's fate.

PBD (pē-bē-dē)

(acro.) Programmer Brain Damage; a label applied to bug reports revealing places where the program was obviously written by an incompetent or short-sighted programmer.

peanut butturbulance (pē'nŭt' bŭ-tûr'byə-ləns)

(n.) The uncontrollable urge to dive into the smooth surface of a freshly opened jar of peanut butter.

2. (n.) The emergency response team that rushes to the aid of someone whose hand got stuck trying to scoop out the last bits of peanut butter from the bottom of a jar.

pedwipe (ped wīp)

(v.) The action of cleaning liquid off the floor with a sock that is still on one's foot because one has run out of paper towels, is too lazy to go get something else to clean it up, or is too lazy to lean over and clean it properly.

PEBKAC (pĕb'kāk)

(acro.) Problem Exists Between Keyboard And Chair; used by support people, particularly at call centers and help desks. Not used with the public. Considered derogatory.

Example: *"Did you ever figure out why that guy couldn't print?" "Yeah, he kept canceling the operation before it could finish. PEBKAC."*

pedlock (pĕd'lŏk')

(n.) The condition when a shoelace winds up in a bicycle pedal or chain, causing bike to stop suddenly, throwing the rider off.

peemiss (pē-mĭs)

(v.) The act of peeing all over the the toilet seat instead of into the bowl.

Example: *If you're too lazy to lift up the seat and peemiss all over it, at least have the courtesy to wipe it up!*

pepsocrust (pĕp-sō-krŭst)

(n.) The hardened and flaky material that encrusts the cap of a tube of toothpaste. This material, although unpleasant, can be used as a last resort when the toothpaste finally runs out.

permafix (pûr'mə-fĭks)

(n.) To permanently fix computer issues of an incompetent user by ripping the power cord from the outlet and taking it, thus preventing future use of the computer.

Example: *He screwed up his computer so badly that I had to apply a permafix.*

permavirgin (pûr'mə-vûr'jĭn)

(n.) One who, because of social awkwardness, inability to be romantic, unattractiveness, or some other reason will remain a virgin forever.

petrifood (pĕt'rə-füd)

(n.) Those rock-hard pieces of food you find behind the couch months after your kids throw them there.

petrophobia (pĕt'rə-fō'bē-ə)

(n.) The fear that one will have to pay for the single cent over-pumped at the self-service station.

pilforkate (pĭl-fôr'kāt')

(v.) To steal food from another person's plate while she is not watching.

pity pile (pĭt'ē pīl)

(n.) An unhappy 2-year-old child who falls into a sobbing heap on the ground in an attempt to play on one's sympathies.

plaquack (plăk'wăk)

(n.) The one mysterious dentist out of five who doesn't provide advice such as recommending sugarless gum for his patients who chew gum.

Origin: From *plaque*, a deposit of hard food particles on one's teeth, and from *quack*, one who pretends to be a physician and provides medical advice.

plotbunny (plŏt'bŭn-ē)

(n.) A tempting idea for a story that hares off into strange territory upon pursuit. Known for breeding rapidly and diverting a writer's attention.

Example: *I've been trying to write a story, but I've been cursed by an infestation of plotbunnies.*

plothole (plŏt-hōl)

(n.) A rough spot in a storyline; a storyline that doesn't quite work, like a pothole is to a road.

plumple (plŭm'pəl)

(n.) A large pimple.

Origin: From *plump* and *pimple*.

See also: *blimple*

poety (pō'ĭt-ē)

(adj.) Poetry-like; something closely resembling the work of a poet. Often used derogatorily to describe bad poetry, rap, and self-indulgent spoken-word sessions.

pointful (point'fəl)

(adj.) To have a point; to be full of good arguments; opposite of pointless.

pooking (pük'ĭng)

(v.) The unfortunate situation in which one must urgently sit on the loo while also vomiting; i.e., it's coming out of both ends.

pooydrink (pü'ē-drĭnk)

(n.) An alcoholic drink that doesn't taste right.

postend (pōst'ĕnd)

(n.) In reference to instant messaging, the window that pops up after one has already closed the conversation, because one assumed the conversation was over 20 minutes ago.

Origin: From *post* and *extend* or *end*.

2. (n.) The last 30 lines of a conversation in which both people want to have the last word and end up saylng goodbye a thousand times.

potentater (pōt'n-tā'tər)

(n.) The largest or longest French fry in a box.

Example: *You can have some of my fries, but you can't have the potentater.*

Origin: From Middle English *potentat*, one who has power over others, and Southern American English *tater*, a potato.

potticize (pŏt'ĭ-sīz)

(v.) To make wild, harebrained, and utterly unfounded hypotheses about everything.

Origin: From *potty*, meaning addled or silly, crazy.

prescribbled (prĭ-skrĭb'əld)

(v.) A method used by doctors with bad handwriting to assign medication to patients.

Example: *My doctor prescribbled me Vexiagasine eye drops but even the pharmacist couldn't read it.*

prestidigitraytion (prĕs'tĭ-dĭj'ĭ-trā'shən)

(n.) The act of quickly trying to remove trash items from a tray on a conveyor belt destined for the great beyond of the cafeteria dishwashing area.

Origin: From French *prestigiateur*, conjurer or juggler, and Old Swedish *trø*, wooden grain measure.

primuctified (prī'mŭk'tə-fīd')

(adj.) Describing a feeling one experiences when one is the first to walk over a freshly mopped floor, often while the janitor looks on.

professore (prə-fĕs'ôr)

(n.) A teacher or educator who doles out copious amounts of tedious homework at his leisure, causing painful calluses on his students' digits.

Origin: From Latin *professus*, professor or teacher, and Old Irish *saeth*, distress or sore.

2. (n.) A teacher or educator who takes sadistic pleasure in the mental anguish of students.

pronuncilexia (prə-nŭn'sə-lĕk'sē-ə)

(n.) A condition in which the sufferer chronically mispronounces words to a high degree, by inserting or omitting sounds after the first letter.

Example: *Those stricken with pronuncilexia sometimes pronounce (among others) "oriented" as "orientated," "carapace" as "carsapace," and "pronounce" as "pronunciate."*

protologism (prō'tŏl'ə-gĭz-əm)

(n.) A newly created word which has not yet gained wide acceptance. This word is self-defining as an example of itself.

Origin: Greek *protos,* first, and Greek *logos,* word. In contrast to *protologisms*, *neologisms* are words that have already been in public usage. In fact, as soon as this very word finds its way into newspapers and websites, journals and books, it will become a *neologism*.

prunles (prü'-nəls)

(n.pl.) The wrinkles that develop on one's fingers when one has been in the water too long.

Origin: From Greek *proumnon*, plum, and from Old English *gewrinclian*, wind or wrinkle.

pseudonymble (süd'nĭm'bəl)

(adj.) The art of juggling multiple online personalities; ability to nimbly juggle many pseudonyms.

Example: *Sally: "I have 13 screen names." John: "You must be very pseudonymble, then!"*

Origin: From *pseudonym*, Greek *pseudonumos*, meaning false name; and *nimble*.

pseudopose (sü'dō-pōz)

(n.) To fake a supposition in lieu of actual knowledge. Also, a random guess for which the purpose is to make the speaker sound more intelligent.

pubicleanse (pyü'bĭ'klĕnz)

(v.) To turn a bar of soap over and over under the hot water tap in a (vain) attempt to remove the one or two curly hairs that are stuck to it.

2. (v.) Fruitless attempt at removing the one curly hair from a bar of soap in the shower, only to gouge out big chunks of the soap, still leaving the hair in place.

punkdunk (pŭngk-dŭngk)

(n.) A flashy or showoff dunk during a basketball game.

pwned (ōnd, pōn, pônd)

(v.tr.) Owned; beaten.

Example: *hahahaha, u got pwned!*

Origin: Used in *leetspeak*, often referring to beating somebody at a game or winning an argument.

Q

quash squash (kwŏsh skwăsh)

(v.tr.) The act of walking on the outer sides of one's feet to dampen the squishing sound of squeaky tennis shoes. Literally, to annul a squishing sound.

quat (kwāt, kwăt)

(v.) Past tense of the verb quit.

quierd (kwîrd)

(adj.) Something that is both queer and weird.

quotimer (kwō-tī-əm'ər)

(n.) One who quotes jokes from one instant messenger conversation into another.

R

radicalotion (răd'ĭ-kəl-ō'shən)

(n.) The aftermath of applying pressure to a clogged bottle of lotion.

randomosity (răn-də-mŏs'ĭ-tē)

(n.) Something displaying the state or quality of being very random.

Origin: Often confused with *insanity*. The difference being that insanity is often involuntary, while *randomosity* is a voluntary choice to do something unexpected.

realizement (rē'ə-līz'mənt)

(n.) A revelation, an epiphany. Something becomes clear or understood after being previously puzzling.

Example: *My realizement is that you are wearing a wig!*

rebootilence (rē-büt-ĕ'ləns)

(n.) The uncomfortable amount of time one has to wait while rebooting one's computer.

2. (n.) Any uncomfortable period of time taken to restart one's computer while one is on the phone with technical support.

rediculadundent (rĭ-dĭk'yə-lə-dŭn-dənt)

(adj.) Having done or said something stupid over and over again.

Example: *Dude, face it; you can't dance. Getting out on the dance floor again would be pretty dang rediculadundent!*

redogdant (rĭ-dōg'dənt)

(adj.) Describing the behavior of naming one's new dog after one's old, and now passed, dog.

Origin: From *redundant* and *dog*.

redonculous (rĭ-dŏng'kyü'ləs)

(adj.) Excessively ridiculous; head-smackingly ridiculous.

Example: *John smacked his head as he exclaimed, "That's redonculous!"*

Origin: A blending of *ridiculous* and *donk*, a dumbfounded bonking of one's head.

See also: *donk*

reflectuate (rĭ-flĕch'ü-āt')

(v.) To fall in love with oneself or one's reflection.

Origin: From *reflect* and *infatuate*.

reflectuous (rĭ-flĕch'ü-əs)

(adj.) Used to describe someone who spends too much time in front of the mirror.

regifter (rē-gĭf'tər)

(n.) One who gives a gift to another that originally was given to oneself.

rememberful (rĭ-mĕm'bər-fəl)

(adj.) Tending to, or likely to remember; antonym to forgetful.

repihumoror (rĕp'ĭ-hyü'mər-ər)

(n.) One who tells the same joke repeatedly to the same people without realizing it, thinking the joke will be funny, again.

2. (n.) One who repeats jokes he or she has seen on television or heard on the radio.

retox (rē-tŏks')

(v.tr.) The act of replenishing toxic substances that have depleted over time.

Example: *Bob wasn't at his desk because he went outside to retox his nicotine levels.*

riceroach (rīs'rōch)

(n.) Any grain of rice in a package of rice that still has its husk.

rippleshot (rĭp'əl-shŏt)

(n.) The ripple marks left on one's skin, usually the face, after waking up from sleeping on wrinkled sheets or pillowcase. Can also come from sleeping on one's watch or anything else that will leave an imprint.

Example: *You have rippleshot all over your arms and face. Perhaps you should remake your bed.*

rizzle (rĭz'əl)

(adj.) Real; true; no kidding.

Example: *That rhyme is fo' rizzle!*

Origin: Likely from terms that originated from rap artist Snoop Dogg, the king of the "izzle."

Roman noodles (rō'mən nüd'ls)

(n.) A noodle dish originating from Rome. More commonly known as spaghetti, ziti, manicotti, and penne, among others.

Origin: A corruption of *ramen noodles*, a traditional Japanese noodle and broth dish.

rotatemate (rŏ'tāt-māt)

(n.) The round swiveling tray used for storing household food items, often holding condiments on your table. Another term for a Lazy Susan.

rubbage (rŭb'ĭj)

(n.) An act of vigorously rubbing a dog's belly while speaking to the dog in baby-talk.

Example: *Oh, does litlte puppy doggy wanna a little rubbage on his belly?*

runawaykey (rŭn-ə'wā-kē)

(n.) Situation where one wakes up late in the morning, realizes one has misplaced one's keys, and is late to work. Often occurs on Mondays.

S

salbaktry (săl-băk-trē)

(n.) The practice of saluting to make a person salute back. Often taken advantage of by second lieutenants who just got their bars.

Example: *That butter bars just got out of OCS, and now he's practicing a little salbaktry by hovering around the door of the enlisted club. What a dork!*

See also: *bowbaktry*

salmon day (săm'ən dā)

(n.) An entire day spent swimming upstream — and then getting skewered and dying in the end.

Example: *I worked on the sales projection for widgets all day, and at 4:30 the boss told me we're dropping the widget line. What a salmon day!*

Sandlersyndrome (sănd'lər-sĭn'drōm')

(n.) One who is fond of quoting lines from Adam Sandler movies and doesn't get sick of it.

Example: *We knew he has Sandlersyndrome when he continually repeated the phrase, "That's pretty sick, Chubbs."*

2. (n.) One who attempts to either duplicate or incorporate the famous Adam Sandler golf swing or batting cage tactics into one's everyday activities.

sapiosexuality (sā-pē-ō-sĕk-shü-ăl'ĭ-tē)

(n.) A behavior of becoming attracted to or aroused by intelligence and its use.

Example: *Me? I don't care too much about the looks. I want an incisive, inquisitive, insightful, irreverent mind. I want someone for whom philosophical discussion is foreplay. I want someone who sometimes makes me go ouch due to their wit and evil sense of humor. I want someone that I can reach out and touch randomly. I want someone I can cuddle with. I decided this all means that I am sapiosexual.*

Origin: From the Latin root *sapien*, wise or intelligent, and Latin *sexualis*, relating to the sexes.

scandroid (skăn'droid')

(n.) The drones who work long hours in the checkout lines scanning items.

Example: *Hey, being a scandroid at Target may not be a glamorous job, but at least I get the employee discount.*

scanter (skăn'tər)

(v.) A brisk, yet leisurely pace. Slower than a gallop, yet faster than a leisurely stroll.

Origin: The combination of a *canter* and a *saunter*.

scantwitch (skăn'twĭch)

(v.) The act of repeatedly trying to scan an item in hopes that one does not have to enter the UPC code by hand.

Origin: The combination of *scan* and *twitch*.

schlitzstop (sh'lǐtz-stŏp)
(n.) The guy who thinks he can drink a beer and play softball at the same time. Often displays a large gut.

schnelling (sh-nĕl-ĭng)
(v.) The act of adding a comically bad German accent; injecting the following words or non-words into conversation: *yah, unst, dah, isnt, yavol, uber, dost*, etc.; adding a *z* sound to any noun.

Example: *Chris was schnelling all evening, saying such things as, "z'telephone ist whreenlng, yah!"*

scholarshipping (skŏl'ər-shǐp'pǐng)
(v.) The act of an organization giving out awards.

Scirish (skī'rǐsh)
(adj.) A person of mixed Irish and Scottish descent.

scoopulate (sküp-yə-lāt')
(v.) The act of pouring a bunch of pills out of a bottle, then scooping up just two of them before pouring the rest back into the bottle.

2. (v.) The act of trying to get only one noodle out of a pot of boiling water to check for doneness.

scrith (skrǐth)
(n.) The narrow lengths of paper one discards after removing the tear-offs of a package or envelope. Likewise, the edges torn off computer paper after discharge from a continuous feed printer.

scrumpled (skrŭm'pəld)

(v.tr.) To make rumpled or appear falling down.

Example: *My socks are scrumpled up.*

Origin: Likely from *scrunched* and *crumpled*.

scrumptuleasant (skrŭmp'shə-lĕz'ənt)

(adj.) Describing a seemingly enjoyable treat that one consumes, but which makes one feel nauseous later.

Example: *That third piece of stuffed pizza tasted great, but 10 minutes later I realized it was scrumptuleasant.*

Origin: A blending of *scrumptious* and *unpleasant*.

seagull (sē'gŭl')

(v.) To enter someone's workplace, make a lot of noise, mess everything up, and then leave. An alternate spelling is "C-gull," in which the "C" refers to "C-level" executives, such as CEO or COO.

seductivity (sĭ-dŭk'tĭv'ĭ-tē)

(n.) A measurement of one's ability to seduce.

seethroughity (sĭ-dŭk'tĭv'ĭ-tē)

(n.) The measure of an object's transparent property, gauged between opaque and completely transparent.

Example: *Professor: "What would you say the seethroughity of this brick wall is?" Student: "I'd say it reads at exactly zero."*

semanticize (sĭ-măn'tĭ-sĭz')

(v.) To start or begin an argument purely over semantics.

Example: *He said I was wrong because I said I have a car, even though I'm just borrowing it. I was not in the mood to semanticize.*

SEO (ĕs-ē-ō)

(acro.) Search Engine Oaf; one who knows absolutely nothing about search engine optimization and other items related to internet marketing and the dealings of internet marketers.

Septleventh (sĕpt-lĕv'ənth)

(n.) The date, September 11th, 2001.

Origin: From the infamous September 11th terrorist attack that destroyed the twin towers and many lives in New York City.

2. (adj.) Any description based on the date, September 11th, 2001.

seriosity (sîr'ē-ŏs'ĭ-tē)

(n.) An amount of seriousness that a given subject measures.

sexile (sĕk'sīl')

(v.) To be banished from one's dorm room or place of residence, as a result of one's roommate engaging in voluptuous activity.

Example: *Josh brought his new girlfriend to our dorm room and sexiled me to the lobby.*

shaffeine (shă-fēn')

(n.) Combination of caffeine and sugar as found in products like Coca-Cola.

Example: *Me need I some shaffeine. I'm up screwing my English.*

shemale (shē'māl)

(n.) A person whose gender is nearly impossible to work out based on physical appearance. One must admit defeat and ask, or sit in viewing distance of both entrances to a public bathroom.

See also: *shim*

shim (shĭm)

(pron.) A pronoun for someone of questionable gender.

2. (n.) A man dressed as a woman.

See also: *shemale*

signoramus (sĭg'nə-rā'məs)

(n.) Someone who drives along in his car unaware that his signal light is flashing. Similarly, one who is ignorant to signals from potential love interests.

siplets (sĭp'lĭts)

(n.pl.) The tiny sips one takes when one's beverage is scalding hot.

shoegating (shü-gāt'ĭng)
(v.) Walking behind someone at a distance too close for comfort, much like tailgating in a car.

siris (sī-rĭs)

(n.) A temptress; a beautiful woman, often an actress, who likely dates so many men that she randomly marries one and divorces within a few months of marriage.

Origin: From Greek *seiren*, siren or temptress, and *iris*, rainbow or assortment.

skeptimistic (skĕp'tə-mĭs'tĭk)

(adj.) Optimistic, yet still skeptical that a particular outcome will occur.

Example: *Raymond was skeptimistic about his team's chances in the big game.*

skrilla (skrĭl'ə)

(n.) Money; cash to be spent freely, not saved.

Example: *I've got to go to work so I can make myself some skrilla.*

sleeky (slēk'ē)

(adj.) A positive, descriptive term referring to anything that is cool. Similar in nature to sleek.

Example: *Your car is so sleeky.*

sloppywords (slŏp'ē-wûrds)

(n.pl.) Words coined and submitted to an online dictionary that are spelled incorrectly or poorly researched.

Example: *Look at all these sloppywords! Half of them are just garbage and the others are already real words.*

slow driving club (slō drīvĭng klŭb)

(n.) A group of cars in front of oneself on the highway that block one from passing while doing exactly the speed limit or even several miles below it.

slowmobile (slō'mō-bēl')

(n.) Any vehicle that turns in front of one's path on the highway and cuts one's traveling speed in half.

sludgatin (slŭj'ə-tn)

(n.) That brown slime found on the top of cafeteria hamburgers.

Example: *The sludgatin on this burger reminds me why I almost never got hot lunch in high school.*

smaste (smāst)

(v.tr.) To taste the way something else smells.

Example: *This smastes like dog food!*

smed (smĕd)

(adj.) Describing an animal that is smelly and dead. Often used in reference to a discovery while one is driving.

Smeed (smēd)

(n.) A nickname for one's cohort; sidekick; right-hand man.

Example: *Smeed, get me something to drink!*

Origin: From old pirate stories. Smeed has often been the name for a captain's sidekick. The name was used primarily in the tale of Peter Pan, in which Captain Hook's sidekick was named Mr. Smeed.

smellifire (směl-ə'fīr)

(v.) To attempt to hide the inevitable bathroom smell one makes by using matches or spray.

Example: *After stinking the bathroom up, James tried to smellifire the room with Lysol.*

2. (n.) One who is caught smellifiring.

smellphone (směl-fōn)

(n.) A person's posterior. Used especially when someone passes wind.

smilder (smǐ'dē)

(adj.) Describing one's toned down smile, especially after displaying a huge, fake smile.

Example: *George, your teeth are blinding! Please be a bit smilder.*

smuffy (smǔf'ē)

(adj.) Used to describe weather that is foggy, cloudy, smoggy, and other forms all combined yet with no precipitation despite the fact that it looks like it will rain at any moment. Often this weather form makes it hard to breathe.

snackrifice (snăk'rə-fīs')

(v.) The act of sharing one's most treasured treat with one's significant other, friend, or family member in order to avoid hurting their feelings or just to be nice.

snagamuffin (snăg'ə-mŭf'ĭn)

(v.) To quickly snatch a muffin or doughnut from the conference room after everyone has left the meeting.

Example: *I forgot my lunch today, so I'm going to snagamuffin as soon as the board meeting ends.*

2. (n.) An affectionate term used in addressing loved ones.

Example: *Ooh, is my widdle snagamuffin sad? Come here and I'll give you a huggy-poo.*

See also: *bitsipookems*

snaktrek (snăk-trĕk)

(n.) A voyage through one's cupboards and refrigerator where no man has gone before in search of a snack.

Example: *My snaktrek was a success: a bag of honey-roasted penuts and two Ho-Hos!*

snapperwrapper (snăp'ər-răp'ər)

(n.) An elastic ponytail holder with a plastic ball at each end. The elastic is wrapped around the ponytail and then one ball is snapped in place over the other.

Origin: Coined by submitter's husband, Terl, after being asked to come up with a better name for her "hair things."

snark attack (snärk ə-tăk')

(n.) A verbal attack from someone who is snarky.

Example: *Watch out for Jane today, unless you're prepared to fend off a serious snark attack.*

sneat (snēt)

(n.) The snow that falls on one's car seat when one opens the car door to get a brush out.

Origin: A combination of *snow* and *seat*.

sniffalist (snĭf-ə-lĭst)

(n.) Any person partaking in the annoying habit of rhythmic sniffing or snorting though free of allergy, cold, or flu. The behavior is a sad attempt to get attention from those within earshot and often precedes speech or movement. Such people can be found in cubicle farms, quiet coffee shops, and university libraries.

snifty (snĭf'tē)

(adj.) The pinnacle of awesome; being both snazzy and nifty.

snormin (snôr'mĭn)

(v.) To snowstorm.

Example: *If it keeps snormin like this, the slopes will be great tomorrow!*

Origin: The contraction of *snowstorming*.

snot rocket (snŏt rŏk'ĭt)

(n.) A gob of mucus that is ejected from either the mouth or nose of a person engaged in a sneeze.

snuggable (snŭg-ə'bəl)

(adj.) Capable of being snuggled; something or someone that is both snuggly and huggable.

solanist (sōl'ə-nǐst)

(n.) A woman who hates men. The female equivalent of a misogynist.

Origin: Adapted from the name of Valerie *Solanas*, who shot and killed Andy Warhol in 1968. She wrote the "SCUM Manifesto" about the non-essential nature of men, whom she considered a "biological accident."

southocity (săüth'ŏs'ĭ-tē)

(n.) A measure of how far south something is.

Example: *Honey, Knoxville is way too far north for spring break. I want to go somewhere with serious southocity, like Key West.*

spamanoia (spăm'ə'noi'ə)

(n.) An abnormal fear of spam, either the junk email variety or the processed canned meat.

spambarrassed (spăm-băr'əsĕd)

(adj.) Feeling ridiculed by an email solicitor about the insufficient size or functionality of one's anatomy.

Example: *I'm not letting that drug company spambarrass me into buying their "anatomy enhancement" medicine.*

spammalogue (spăm'ə-lŏg)

(n.) An unsolicited, unwanted, and one-sided series of emails, usually concerning romantic hopes or business pursuits. Most common in cases of heartbreak.

Origin: From *spam* and *monologue*.

spanks (spăngks)
(interj.) A sarcastic expression of thanks.

Example: *Spank you for doing the laundry — and using up all the detergent!*

spanktervision (spăngk'tər-vĭzh'ən)
(n.) Raunchy television that normally airs after midnight on cable networks, X-rated pay-per-view, and cable television.

spendorphine (spĕn-dôr'fĭn)
(n.) The substance generated by the brain that improves mood or reduces depression when one self-medicates by going shopping.

Example: *Ahh, two hours in Macy's and an hour in the shoe stores. The spendorphines are flowing!*

spirly (spûr'lē)
(adj.) Crazy, insane, a little off; special.

Example: *Taz is quite spirly this evening.*

Origin: The accidental love-child of *spinny* and *twirly*.

splitzophrenic (splĭt'sə-frĕn'ĭk)
(adj.) A personality trait that causes a person to consistently behave in an inconsistent manner. Common symptoms include extreme indecisiveness and frequent shifting between hyper, impulsive, and spastic behavior and a more subdued, introspective demeanor. Victims sway between the following traits: extroverted vs. introverted, practical/ realistic vs. imaginative, organized vs. disorganized, intelligent/clearheaded vs. ditsy, stubborn vs. complacent, among others.

sprolic (sprô'lĭk)

(v.) To frolic and splash in puddles or snow.

spurgle (spûr'gəl)

(v.) The sputtering and gurgling sound a car sometimes makes after the ignition is turned off.

spyawn (sp'yôn)

(v.) To attempt to speak while yawning.

2. (n.) Any instance of talking and yawning simultaneously.

squeats (skwēts)

(n.pl.) The feeling resulting from a need to use the restroom when you're doing some more important. This usually results in squirming in your seat.

Example: *I gotta go bad, but I know the best part of this movie is coming up. I guess I'll just have to deal with the squeats.*

squibbly (skwĭb'əl'ē)

(adj.) Tiny; small; minute; a small piece of something.

Example: *Hey, just give me a squibbly piece of your cake and I'll stop begging.*

squoze (skwōz)

(v.tr.) To have squeezed something previously. The past tense of squeeze.

Example: *Yes, I squoze it as hard as I could but I couldn't get any more juice out of the lime.*

starvatious (stär'vā'shəs)

(adj.) Suffering from a severe feeling of hunger.

Example: *Robert, I know you want to get to Pennsylvania before it gets dark, but can we please stop to eat? We're all starvatious!*

stilby (stĭl-bē)

(n.) A mullet. Short top, long back.

Example: *That field hockey player is rocking a serious stilby!*

Origin: From *STLB*; short top, long back.

stopengawker (stŏp'n'gôk'ər)

(n.) A motorist who slows down to watch a curious event, causing a traffic jam, thus adding to the problem.

stoptional (stŏ'shə-nəl)

(adj.) When stopping at a stop sign is left to choice.

2. (adj.) Any stop sign with a white border.

Note: For your own safety, please stop at all stop signs, and look in both directions.

stries (strīz)

(n.pl.) The stray fries in the bottom of a fast food bag.

See also: *fryfugee* and *fugifries*

stuffilated (stŭf'ĭ-lāy-tĕd)

(v.tr.) Eating to the point where it's difficult to move.

Example: *They stuffilated themselves at the buffet.*

stupedious (stü'pē'dē-əs)

(adj.) Describing something that is both stupid and tedious.

Example: *Oh, why does John always assign all the stupedious taks to me? Can't he get an intern to do them?*

stupicide (stü'pĭ-sīd')

(n.) Unintentionally killing oneself by attempting a stupid stunt, such as trying to jump off a roof and land in the pool.

Example: *He committed stupicide by mounting a jet engine to his moped.*

stupiculous (stü-pĭk'yə-ləs)

(adj.) Stupidly ridiculous.

sturp (stûrp)

(n.) The last bead of toothpaste remaining behind the nozzle of the tube; often it cannot be reached.

Origin: Possibly from *stubborn* and *-p* from either *paste* or the initials *TP* for toothpaste.

stylephile (stīl-fīl')

(n.) A person who is obsessive about current fashions.

Example: *Sure, Crickett is a stylephile, but she always dresses great.*

Origin: From *style*, fashion, and *-phile*, having an affinity for.

submiss (səb-mĭs)

(v.) To click a "submit" button that fails to work.

suffixification (sŭf'ĭks-ĭ'fĭ-kā'shən)

(n.) The process by which an unword is made by adding a suffix to a real word.

Example: *realizement*

sulduxy (sŭl'dŭk-sē)

(adj.) Describing that which is sultry, seductive, and sexy.

summer teeth (sŭm'ər tēth)

(n.) Teeth that do not grow in a uniform direction, such that some are here and some are there.

Example: *Yeah, Jack is cute, but a little orthodonia would take care of those summer teeth.*

's up (sŭp)

(abbrev.) The question, "What's up?"

Example: *'S up, yo?*

superflugraph (su-pûr'flü-grăf)

(n.) Meaningless pictures taken just to use up the end of the roll of film.

Origin: From *superfluous* and *photograph*.

superfluswitch (sü-pûr'flü-swĭch)

(n.) The one light switch in every house with absolutely no purpose whatsoever.

Origin: From *superfluous* and *switch*.

Example: *"Honey, what is this switch for?" "Oh, the Realtor said that was just the house's mandatory superfluswitch."*

supposibly (sə-pŏs'ə-blē)

(adv.) Describing something that is supposedly possible.

Example: *Conan supposibly could break a world record, but he's far to lazy to do so.*

swankienda (swăng'kē-ěn'də)

(n.) An extremely nice house.

Example: *Tom's house — which has nine bedrooms and a 6,000-square-foot game room — is quite a swankienda.*

Origin: Combination of *swanky*, *fancy*, and *hacienda*, a large estate in Spanish-speaking countries.

sweave (swēv)

(v.) To swerve and weave about. Often used by drunks attempting to drive.

Example: *Brian: "What? Why are you giving me a ticket, officer?" Policeman: "Sir, you were sweaving all over the road. Clearly you're drunk."*

swish-swash (swĭsh-swôsh)

(adj.) The tendency to leave one's windshield wipers on even after the rain has stopped.

syntheticity (sĭn-thě'tĭs'ĭ-tē)

(n.) An object's state of being synthetic. As opposed to organicity.

Example: *Dude, I don't care what the saleslady told you. The syntheticity of the "leather" on your new sneakers is 100 percent.*

T

tacois (täcō-ĭz)

(v.) The act of using someone else's online messaging system to trick people into thinking they are talking to the actual owner of the account.

Example: *I'm going to tacois Ajus the next time he leaves his desk.*

Origin: The accidental birth of a term that somewhat resembles *take over*, which originated from a mistyping of the phrase, "do you like tacos," while doing the act itself.

Tandy (tăn'dē)

(adj.) Used to describe any computer or electronic gadget that is particularly lame or obsolete.

Origin: *Tandy* was a computer sold by Radio Shack starting in 1980.

tangentalize (tăn-jĕn'tə-līz')

(v.) To go off on a tangent or bunny trail in a conversation.

tangentman (tăn-jĕn't-măn)

(n.) Any individual prone to suddenly changing the current subject of discussion without warning or due cause. This is usually done to bring the discussion to a subject either close to the tangentman's heart, or to make the tangentman the center of the discussion.

Example: *Dan: "Did you see the match last night?" Harry: "Yes, I thought it was a really close game, but the ref lost it a bit towards the end." Jacob: "I'm going to the dentist tomorrow." Dan and Harry: "Tangentman strikes again!"*

the **UnWord DICTIONARY** **163**

tanggold (tang'gold)

(v.tr.) When two or more gold chains myteriously get tangled after one puts them on one's neck or wrist and does nothing else. Before one knows it, they're tanggold.

tape scrape (tāp skrāp)

(v.) The act of clawing and scratching at a roll of scotch tape to pull up the end when the one who used it last let the tape adhere to itself.

tapz (tăpz)

(n.pl.) Really awkward or outlandish shoes; shoes thought to be on the cutting edge of new fashion.

Origin: From *taps*, originally metal plates set into the heels for tap-dancing and now referencing shoes in general.

tar circles (tär sûr'kəls)

(n.pl.) Strange circles and other shapes found etched into a road that are sometimes believed to be created by flying saucers.

Origin: From *crop circles*.

teamlet (tēm'lĭt)

(n.) A team within a larger team. Consisting of as few as one member, teamlets can research topics of great importance and report back to a team or larger teamlet which reports to an even larger team.

Example: *OK Frank, you research the new media platform and report back to the publishing teamlet next week.*

tearyold (tîr'ē-ōld)

(adj.) Descriptive of the act of a two-year-old child throwing a tantrum.

teenanswer (tēn-ăn'sər)

(n.) Any answer to a question that doesn't properly address the question, like those of a teenager.

Example: *Question: "What are you doing?" Teenanswer: "He started it!"*

teh (tĕ)

(art.) Slang. The.

Example: *"Teh mail is here."*

Origin: A deliberate misspelling used to make fun of someone's typo(s). Generally associated with electronics or the Internet, the most common origin of typos.

teletalktic (tel'ə-tôk'tĭk)

(adj.) Describing one who talks frequently on the phone.

tellum (tĭ'lŭm)

(n.) The complete opposite of a mullet — short in the back, long in the front.

the ness (thə nĕs)

(n.) A series of positive or complimenting words that all end in "ness," like greatness, coolness, awesomeness, sweetness, sexiness, etc.

Example: *That party last Saturday was the ness.*

teleflector (tĕl'ĭ-flĕk'tər)

(n.) One who uses a television in its off position as a mirror.

2. (n.) The television used as a mirror.

throatee (thrō'tē)

(n.) Term describing the style of only growing the hair on one's face from below the chin throughout the neck and shaving all other facial hair.

Origin: From *goatee*.

thrux (thrŭks)

(n.) The absolute core and driving force behind something.

Example: *Education is the thrux of this labor government's manifesto.*

Origin: A contraction of the words *thrust* and *crux*.

thumbulate (thŭm'yə-lāt')

(v.) To lean forward while pressing the buttons on the remote hoping that the extra inch will make the remote control work better.

2. (v.) To push harder on a button in hopes that it will revive a remote with clearly dead batteries.

Example: *You've been thumbulating that remote for three days. Face it, it's not going to work right until you install new batteries!*

tictactic (tĭk-tăk-tĭk)

(n.) A technique used to try to get one tic-tac from its container.

Example: *I always get two out every time; I should really look into using a new tictactic.*

toe cleavage (tō klē'vĭj)

(n.) The result of women's footwear that is cut too deeply along the top of the foot, showing where the toes begin, but not the entire toe.

Origin: Similar to a low cut top showing chest cleavage.

tonsil boxing (tŏn'səl bŏksĭng)

(v.) The act of passionate, open mouthed French kissing; to make out.

trafficated (trăf'ĭ-kāt'ĕd)

(v.tr.) A state in which the roads are packed so full of traffic that it is beyond what normal bad traffic can describe.

Origin: A play on *traffic* and *constipated*, suggesting the roads are clogged up.

See also: trafficy

trafficy (trăf'ĭk'ē)

(adj.) Describing a period of heightened traffic.

Example: *Dang, it's trafficy today. We're never going to make it to the movie on time.*

See also: trafficated

transvert (trăns-vûrt')

(n.) A psychological type that alternates between introversion and extroversion and combines features of both types.

Example: *His life moves from one extreme to another, from complete self-absorption to wild partying at random places with random people. He is a typical transvert.*

tree rat (trē răt)

(n.) A squirrel; a very destructive animal that eats bird eggs—contributing more to the demise of song birds than even house cats.

treeware (trē'wâr')

(n.) Hacker slang. Documentation or other printed material.

Origin: Like *software* or *hardware*, *tree* suggests a type of ware for computers that is of a tree form.

trevel (trĕv'əl)

(n.) Merry-making while on the move.

2. (v.in.) To indulge in boisterous revelry whilst going from one place to another.

Origin: The blending of *travel* and *revel*, to take pleasure in.

tripendicular (trī'pən-dĭk'yə-lər)

(adj.) The disorienting view one has while falling or moving in an arc, or in a direction other than horizontal or vertical.

Example: *They traveled tripendicularly on the roller coaster.*

Origin: A combination of *perpendicular* and *parallel*.

trubbleyu (trŭb'əl-yü)

(n.) The coolest way to say "www," the beginning of most web addresses.

tubarine (tŭb'ə-rēn')

(n.) A margarine tub.

turcreation (tûr'krē-ā'shən)

(v.) The process by which Thanksgiving turkey leftovers multiply in the refrigerator to a seemingly infinite quantity.

Example: *I figured we'd have Thanksgiving leftovers for a couple of days, but turcreation has created another week's worth.*

turfus (tur'fəs)

(n.pl.) A repellent and often unidentifiable mass, as of sweaty clothes or food waste.

Example: *When Jeff moved out, he left such nasty turfus under his couch that I had to use gloves to throw it out.*

Origin: From *turf*, a layer of sod and possibly British slang, to displace or eject.

twitterpated (twĭt'ər-pāt'ĕd)

(adj.) Describing someone who is head over heels in love.

Origin: From *twitter*, to utter in chirps expressing overwhelming excitement, and from *-pate*, of the head or brain.

U

UBD (yü-bē-dē)

(acro.) User Brain Damage; an abbreviation used to close out trouble reports originally created because of a clueless user's misunderstanding.

überize (ü-bûr-īz')

(v.) To tack the German prefix "über" (meaning really, very, or super) to any English word to make it sound cool.

Example: *I've überized cool, freaky, and wild. They are now über-cool, über-freaky, and über-wild.*

umfriend (ŭm-frĕnd)

(n.) An intimate relation of dubious standing or a concealed voluptuous relationship.

Example: *This is Pat, my ... umfriend.*

unanimosity (yü-năn'ə-mŏs'ĭ-tē)

(n.) The result when everyone is in agreement, but nobody likes what they agreed upon.

Origin: The contraction of *unanimous*, sharing the same opinion, and *animosity*, expressing bitter hatred toward.

unbelievabubble (ŭn'bĭ-lē-və-bŭb'əl)

(adj.) Excellently good; excellently fantabulous.

Origin: From *unbelievable*, incredible or beyond lucky, and *abubble*, excited.

undocumentioned (ŭn-dŏk'yə-mĕn'shən'ĕd)

(adj.) Describing something that is both undocumented and unmentionable.

Example: *Don't tell me about the offshore accounts, they're undocumentioned!*

undysfunctionalize (ŭn'dĭs-fŭngk'shən-ə'lĭz')

(v.) To get family counseling.

Example: *My parents and I got along a lot better after three sessions of undysfunctionalizing.*

Uneasytarian (ŭn-ē'zē-târ'ē-ən)

(n.) Usually middle-class suburban parents who come from different religious backgrounds, Uneasytarians participate in no specific religion but have a fuzzy belief in God. Uneasytarians are distinguished by their constant guilt and waffling over whether or not to send their children to church or provide them with some sort of spiritual background.

Example: *I was raised by a pair of Uneasytarians (a lapsed Catholic and a Methodist with little conviction) and they expressed constant regret that their daughter had grown up to be an atheist. "We could have taken you to church if you'd only asked!" they cried, wringing their hands.*

unfhair (ŭn'fâr')

(adj.) Marked by the ability to grow hair on one's ears, nose, the back of one's neck, on one's back or on one's rear, but not on the top of one's own head.

unsermonizable (ŭn-sûr'mə-nīz'ə-bəl)

(adj.) Possessing a resistance to religious instruction.

Example: *I told my girlfriend I'm unsermonizable, but she still tries to get me to go to church with her.*

unsmile (ŭn-smīl)

(v.in.) The transition from a smile to a more neutral expression.

Example: *John smiles through the day, but whenever he passes a policeman he unsmiles.*

unstaple (ŭn-stā'pəl)

(n.) A staple that doesn't go all the way through the pages.

Example: *The last three pages of my term paper fell off and landed in the mud because of that darn unstaple!*

untake (ŭn-tāk)

(v.) To put something back; to separate.

untruthitude (ŭn-trüth'ĭ-tüd')

(n.) A boldfaced lie.

Example: *Jason told a real untruthitude when he reported that there was no poverty problem despite all the homeless people wandering about behind him.*

Origin: From *untruth* and *attitude*.

unultimationer (ŭn-ŭl'tə-mā-shən-ər)

(n.) One who thinks he is the best, but who is considered a joke or cheesy to others.

Origin: From English *ultimation*, of or relating to being ultimate or superior, and Latin *ultimus* farthest, last. In this case, "farthest from superior."

unword (ŭn'wûrd)

(n.) An imaginary word, or a word that was made up to give meaning to something.

2. (n.) A sound or combination of sounds in written form that communicates a meaning that is not accepted as part of a language, but was made up to communicate a meaning that otherwise does not exist or is unknown to a particular language.

unwordaphobia (ŭn'wûrd-ə-fō'bē-ə)

(n.) A state in which one is scared of any word that is not in the dictionary.

Example: *My English prof has a major case of unwordaphobia. If we write a word that's not in the OED, she takes 10 points off!*

unwordiwitafulliphilophobia (ŭn-wûrd-ĭ-wĭt'ĭ-ful'ĭ-fī'lō-fō'bē-ə)

(n.) Fear of becoming so obsessed with using unwords in a conversation that friends will shun this person from the "circle" for trying too hard to be witty. Fear of being incomprehensible for trying to be witty through the excessive use of unwords that no one else knows.

Example: *I love using unwords, but when I'm among people I don't know well, unwordiwitafulliphilophobia strikes me.*

Origin: A blending of *unword, wit, awfully, philo-,* and *phobia.* The use of *philo-* in this context means dear or friendly.

unwordly (ŭn'wûrd'lē)

(adj.) That which cannot be adequately described by using any words in an "official" dictionary.

Example: *Some sentiments are simply unwordly; that's why we have The Unword Dictionary.*

ush (ŭsh)

(v.) The act of escorting. Ushers partake in the act of ushing.

Example: *You were supposed to be ushing at church today! Hopefully someone else ushed for you.*

V

varidextrous (vâ'rĭ-dĕk'strəs)

(adj.) Neither right-handed or left-handed; performs some tasks with the right hand and others with the left. Similar to *ambidextrous*, but different in that an ambidextrous person can use either hand equally well, while a varidextrous person does some things better with the left hand and other things better with the right.

Example: *Josh is varidextrous — he bats right-handed, pitches left-handed, and signs autographs right-handed.*

varietous (və-rī'ĭ-təs)

(adj.) Having great variety.

Example: *I love shopping at this bakery on Saturday morning. The coffeecakes are so varietous!*

vendage (věn'děj)

(n.) The age, usually unknown, of over-processed food items found in common vending machines.

Example: *I'm pretty hungry, but the food in this machine is of questionable vendage.*

Origin: A combination of *vend* and *vintage*.

verbal-vomit (vûr'bəl-vŏm'ĭt)

(n.) Spontaneous comments that make no sense, have no point, or are completely off the subject.

Viday (vī-dāy)

(n.) Virtual Friday, which occurs when one's last day of work for the week is not on Friday.

Example: *Frank is off Thursday and Friday for Thanksgiving, so Wednesday is his Viday.*

videocracy (vĭd'ē-ŏk'rə-sē)

(n.) The power of visual images in shaping contemporary societies; the crucial impact of television, cinema, internet, and advertising on public opinion, political affairs, market strategies, etc.

Example: *Ideocracy is dead. The so-called communist countries are communist no longer. Was it the power of democratic ideals or American-style videocracy that ended the communist utopia? Perhaps videocracy has become an indispensable part of democracy in the media age.*

viewlexia (vyü-lĕk'sē-ə)

(n.) Temporary dysfunction in which a novice digital camera user puts her eye very close to the LCD screen as if it were the viewfinder in a conventional camera.

vigilauntie (vĭj'əl-än'tē)

(n.) The relative in every family who is snoopy and always poking her nose into other people's business.

Example: *I know my vigilauntie means well, but if she doesn't stop nagging me to get a "real" job, I'm going to explode. After all, being a webmaster is a real job!*

Origin: From *vigilante* and *auntie*.

virii (vī-rē)

(n.pl.) More than one virus. Usually relating to having more than one virus on one's computer.

Example: *I can't wait to get home and use my Mac. All the dang virii on this PC at work make it impossible to get anything done.*

voguenoxious (vōg-nŏk'shəs)

(adj.) The state of being stylish or in vogue, to the point of being annoying to others. To be obnoxious about one's own style.

voilissimo (vwä-lē-sē'mō)

(interj.) To play in a diligently excellent way.

Origin: From French *voila*, expressing satisfaction, and the root *-issimo* from words like *pianissimo* and *fortissimo*.

voluntold (vŏl'ən-tōld)

(v.) When one has been volunteered for something by another person, often against one's wishes or desires.

Example: *My mom voluntold me to help at Aunt Muriel's wedding.*

Origin: From *volunteer* and *told*.

vomitous (vŏm'ĭ-təs)

(adj.) Describing a situation or thing that causes one to feel like vomiting.

2. (adj.) Prone to spewing; not necessarily vomit, but also words, stories, advice, negativity, etc.

Example: *Every morning I dread it when Jackie comes into my office to vent about her latest "horrible" problem. She's the most vomitous person I know.*

vu jadé (vü zhä'dā)

(n.) The strange feeling that an experience has never happened before.

vurp (vûrp)

(v.) To be reminded of what had been eaten last via a short belch-like occurrence.

Example: *That pizza tasted great last night, but I didn't need that vurp to remind me of it.*

2. (n.) A vomit burp.

W

w00t (wüt)

(interj.) See *woot.* An alternate spelling used to exclaim one's leet-speak abilities.

Example: *W00t! I'm uber-1337! I just g0t 4 h34dsh0ts. I am teh g0d.*

wafflence (wŏf'ə'ləns)

(n.) An inability to make up one's mind.

Example: *Knock off the wafflence, man. Are you going jogging with us or not?*

Origin: From *waffle,* slang for indecisive.

waffy (wŏ'fē)

(adj.) A feeling of emotional unwellness that cannot be categorized as anger, sadness, loneliness, and the like. May be produced by mild PMS.

Example: *Yeah, I know I said I wanted to go out for pizza, but now I'm feeling really waffy and just want to stay in my dorm room.*

Origin: Likely a corruption of *waft* and *woozy*.

wafro (wă-frō)

(n.) A Caucasian individual with tight curly hair.

Origin: From *afro,* a tight curly hair style of African origin, and *white.*

WAM (wăm)

(v.) To review printed material quickly, looking for obvious errors. Process usually used by editors.

Example: *Before the catalog goes to press, I want to WAM it one more time.*

Origin: Based on the procedures used by employees of the U.S. Bureau of Printing and Engraving, mainly the Women At the Mint (WAM), who visually scan the sheets of uncut money for mistakes.

waspafarian (wŏs'pŭ-făr-ē'ən)

(adj.) A white guy or girl with dreadlocks.

Origin: From the slang term *WASP*, a white anglo-saxon protestant, and the faith *rastafarian*.

weaselocity (wē'zə-lŏs'ĭ-tē)

(n.) Being weasely; like a weasel. A measure of one's weasely behavior.

Example: *You jerk! You're the epitome of weaselocity!*

webaholic (wĕ'bə-hôl'ĭk)

(n.) One who is uncontrollably addicted to surfing the Internet, visiting websites or otherwise making use of the Internet.

webbiage (wĕb-bĭj)

(n.) Excessive use of web tools and design beyond those needed to present content or achieve a certain goal.

Example: *Why do you need all this webbiage? Simplify, simplify!*

Whenterday (wĕn'tər-dā)

(n.) A handy word used when one wants to specify a day of the week.

Example: *Jane: "Whenterday will it be done?" Jack: "Most likely Sunday."*

Origin: The combination of *whenever* and *day*.

whinese food (hwī'nēz füd)

(n.) North American corruption of Chinese food. Transitioning ethnic Chinese food into American cuisine.

Example: *When Sam came back from foreign study in Beijing, he couldn't stand the whinese food we think is typical Chinese.*

Whitesican (wīt'sĭ-kən)

(n.) Someone of Caucasian and Mexican heritage.

wickcellent (wĭk'sə-lənt)

(interj.) Being both wicked (in the awesome sense of the word) and excellent. Used when one word alone will not suffice for an exclamation.

Example: *That Halloween costume you made out of an old sheet is wickcellent, dude!*

woof (wuf)

(acro.) Well Off Older Folk.

Example: *Aren't they just a bunch of woofs, driving their golf carts down the sidewalk.*

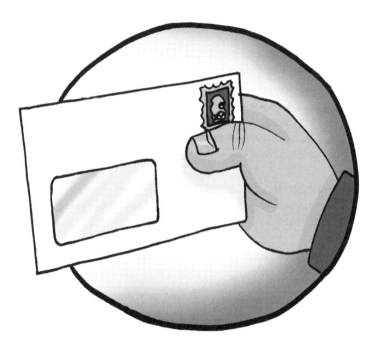

winvelope (wĭn'və-lōp)
  (n.) Any fancy envelope with an address window cutout.
  Any dual-pane envelope that includes a return address
  window.

woot (wüt)

(interj.) Celebratory exclamation used especially in online role-playing games.

Example: *Woot! I gained a level!*

2. (acro.) We Owned Other Team. Alternatively spelled w00t or w007.

Origin: Initially used by gamers to express victory via landslide, now its meaning has been generalized to express accomplishment.

word-donor (wûrd dō'nər)

(n.) One who has created one or more words; one who has contributed original words to a dictionary.

worddork (wûrd-dôrk)

(n.) One who stays up til 4:30 in the morning thinking of words that don't exist.

wordematician (wûrd'ə-mə-tĭsh'ən)

(n.) The occupation or title of one who creates words.

Origin: From a combination of *word* and *mathematician*.

wordish (wûrd-ĭsh)

(adj.) Describing an unword used in speech that resembles existing words.

Example: *"Is retardulous even a word?" "It's wordish."*

wordjones (wŭrd'jōnz'ĕz)

(n.pl.) Describes anyone with the desire to coin new words.

worrification (wûr'ĭfĭ-kā-shŭn)

(n.) State of being worried.

wuzgonna (wŭz'gŭn'ə)

(v.tr.) The intention to complete a task prior to thinking of an excuse or reason not to complete said task.

Example: *I wuzgonna go jogging but decided to take a nap instead.*

X

xyzed (ĕks-wī-zēd)

(v.in.) To have examined one's own pant zipper to see if it was unzipped.

2. (v.in.) For one to have been examined to see if his pants were unzipped.

Origin: From eXamine Your Zipper. Out of common decency, using *xyzed* allows one to be informed without taking the full weight of embarrassment that would come with being told out loud that they are unzipped.

3. (v.in.) To have been filled in on important information known to everyone else but oneself.

Y

yaaow (yăü')

(interj.) Yo; hey; used to call attention to something.

yabut (yĕ'ə-bŭt)

(conj.) Yes, however. Argumentative form.

Example: *Mom: "Nate, didn't you say you were going to do your homework before the movie?" Nate: "Yabut, I got busy updating my Facebook page."*

Origin: From *yeah* and *but*.

yeahno (yĕ'ə-nō)

(adv.) Being affirmative while at the same time covering the opposite possibility. Particularly favored by sportspeople during game time when it appears as though their team is going to score a point.

yimes (yīms)

(interj.) An expression of shock or awe.

Example: *Yimes! My phone bill this month is ginormous!*

Origin: The contraction of *yikes* and *blimey*, two expressions of surprise.

yippideehooha (yĭp'ĭ-dē-hü'hä)

(n.) The ruckus of media — including commentary, interviews, and highlights — which follow the winning of any major sports championship. Similarly: (pl.) yippidee-hoohas, yippideeprehas (fanfare preceding the big game), yippideeposthas.

Example: *We don't need to listen to anymore of this yippideehooha. We already know who won the game.*

Origin: Most likely a by-blow taken from the movie *Song of the South*, featuring the song "Zip-A-Dee-Doo-Dah."

2. (n.) The media excitement over any major news event and the continued "coverage" that ensues.
3. (n.) The excessive media coverage on a news event that is of extremely low importance.

youing (yü'ĭng)

(contr.) Short for "you going."

Example: *Youing my way?*

Origin: Inspired by common abbreviations like "you are" to "you're" and "it is" to "it's."

youness (yü-nəs)

(n.) The second person form of oneness.

Example: *You must be in youness with yourself.*

2. (n.) The state of being one's self.
3. (n.) The unique quality of being one's self. Unique qualities usually include: personality, personal tendencies, looks.

youthemism (yüth'ə-mĭz'əm)

(n.) Any story or term invented for the purpose of explaining to a young child a concept or phenomenon that he or she is too young to properly understand.

Example: *Dad: "The stork brought you and left you in a basket on our front portch, sweetie." Jane: "Dad, I'm 12 now. You don't need to give me that youthemism any more."*

Z

zipply (zĭp'lē)

(adv.) Quickly; to do something in a zip or with a sharp hissing sound; to act in a swift fashion.

Example: *George, can you zipply fax this 200-page document for me? Thanks! This will be so great.*

zit spit (zĭt spĭt)

(n.) The ooze that comes forth from a zit when it breaks.

zoodles (zü-dəls)

(n.) Lots of; a large amount.

Example: *Thanks mum. I have zoodles of spaghetti to eat.*

zoozoo (zü-zü)

(n.) A person who sits at a desk all day long.

Origin: Possibly relating to the 1913 definition of *zoozoo*, the wood pigeon; may infer a derogatory reference toward those with desk jobs.

The Neologians

The author would like to acknowledge the following people, who contributed words to The Unword Dictionary.

Anonymous

Aharon Boheman

Aidan B.

Amy Ulery

Andrew Wyant

Anne R.

Ashley

Athena Hellsing

Ben Botwin

Ben Gross

Benjamin Kempf

Bob Smith

Brent Blasingim

Brian Szmyd

Brianne Gregory

Brittney McKenna

Carlos Villa

Carol Sexton

Catherine Lambe

Chelsea Powell

Chelsea Porter

Christopher Schneider

Christopher Martin

Christopher Jenquin

Cynthia Young

Danielle Bacon

Dave Balmer

Dominique Gurra

Doug Pinch

Drew Jackson

Eddie Fitzgerald

Elaine Rauser

Elisha Baker

Emily Gomez

Emily Ulery

Ferdinangus

Fergus Power

FK Funderburke

Fred Sawtelle

Gabriel Bider

Geoffrey Ludwig

Grania's Bard

Igor Kaplounenko

J Biers

Jack Holmes

Jarrod Dogg

Jason Clark Laidlaw

Jason Dries

Jen Collins

Jenifer Strickland

Jennifer Reed

Jerry Serafine

Jill Kleinowski

Jim Bob

Joe Ford

Joe Cushing

Joe Caston

Joey Oddo

John Cummings

John Wheeler

John Shupe

John Heyworth

John Brown

Joseph Papke

Joy McCroskey

Karen Robinson

Katherine Naini

Kathy Shaull

Katie Carter

Kelsey Rose

Kendra Gathers

Kenneth Lee

Kevin McCall

Kiyoshi Odo

Kris Jeters

Kukkuroa Uvaca

Kylee Nugent

Lauren Linder

Leah Nottellin

Lee Perry

Liam Fletcher

Lisa Rea

Louie Simpson

Lynda Smith

Marc Bagnell

Marc LaCounte

Marcelo Leal

Marcey Rhyne

Mason Ponsonby

Matthew Ryan

Mawm Mom

Michael Oiga

Michael von Plato

Michael Sussman

Michael Turley

Mick Synnott

Mikhail Epstein

Mori Bellamy

Myke Cole

Nicholas Nonya

Nick L.

Nicole Smith

P. Edwards

Paraphelion Corquescant

Raoul Widman

Rich Hamilton

Richard Vodden

Rob Weathers

Robert Evans

Robert Randolph

Ryan Burkett

Sally Shane

Simon Croker

Stacey Sevilla

Stephen Gill

Steve Kiehl

Svetlana Mati

T. S.

Thomas Millington

Tim Kang

Tom

Victoria Mabry

Vivienne Barter

Voltron

Yasmin Martin

If you enjoyed The Unword Dictionary, you'll love the other titles in the How America Speaks Series from Marion Street Press, Inc.

Buy them today from your favorite book retailer.

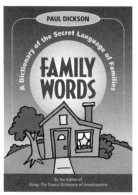